Wisdom With Understanding is Better Than Rubies

Lurine Karon Greenberg Fine Arts Collection

VIOLIN PLAYING
As I Teach It

VIOLIN PLAYING
As I Teach It

LEOPOLD AUER

Dover Publications, Inc.
New York

This Dover edition, first published in 1980, is an un-
abridged and unaltered republication of the edition published by J. B. Lippincott Company, Philadelphia, in
1960. (The original edition was published by Frederick
A. Stokes Company, N.Y., in 1921; in its original typo-
graphic form, the book was later published by J. B. Lippincott Company as "A Stokes Book.")

International Standard Book Number: 0-486-23917-9
Library of Congress Catalog Card Number: 79-55749

Manufactured in the United States of America
Dover Publications, Inc.
31 East 2nd Street, Mineola, N.Y. 11501

CONTENTS

Chapter		Page
	PREFACE	vii
	INTRODUCTION	ix
I	HOW I STUDIED THE VIOLIN	1
II	HOW TO HOLD THE VIOLIN	10
	The Violin	10
	The Position of the Thumb	11
	The Bow	12
III	HOW TO PRACTISE	14
IV	TONE PRODUCTION	18
	Some Hints on the Subject of Tone Production	20
	The *Vibrato*	22
	The *Portamento* or *Glissando*	24
V	HINTS ON BOWING	26
	The *Détaché* (Detached Stroke)	26
	The *Martelé* (Hammer-Stroke)	26
	The *Staccato* Up-and-Down Bow	27
	The *Staccato Volant* ("Flying *Staccato*")	28
	The *Spiccato Sautillé* (*Spiccato* with Bouncing, Springing Bow)	28
	The *Ricochet-Saltato* (Rebound with Springing Bow)	29
	The *Tremolo*	30
	The Arpeggio	30
	The *Legato*	31
VI	LEFT-HAND TECHNIQUE	34
	The Change of Positions	34
	The Pressure of the Fingers on the Strings	36
	Scales and Other Exercises	37
	Chromatic Scales	39
	Fingering	40

v

CONTENTS

Chapter		Page
VII	DOUBLE-STOPS—THE TRILL	45
	Scales in Thirds	45
	Scales in Fourths	46
	Scales in Sixths	48
	Simple Octaves (1–4 Fingers)	48
	Fingered Octaves	49
	Tenths	50
	The Trill	50
	Three- and Four-Note Chords	53
VIII	ORNAMENTS—*Pizzicato*	54
	Pizzicato	56
IX	HARMONICS	58
	Natural Harmonics	58
	Artificial Harmonics	58
	Double Harmonics	59
X	NUANCE—THE SOUL OF INTERPRETATION—PHRASING	61
	Phrasing	70
XI	STYLE	74
XII	THE NERVES AND VIOLIN PLAYING	85
XIII	THE VIOLIN REPERTORY OF YESTERDAY AND TODAY	89
XIV	PRACTICAL REPERTORY HINTS	96
	What I Give My Pupils to Play	96

PREFACE

Iɴ the following pages I have tried, as best I could, to give the serious teacher and student the practical benefit of the knowledge I have acquired during a long life devoted to playing and teaching the violin. I have here endeavoured not only to make clear my ideas and ideals regarding the art, but to explain the mechanical means, and technical procedure, which I myself have used in developing my pupils, in the hope and belief that what I have written may be of help to all students who are sincerely and honestly trying to become masters of that wonderful instrument—the violin.

I have simply and frankly endeavoured to explain the art of violin playing as well-nigh sixty years of experience as an interpreting artist and teacher have revealed it to me. My advice, my conclusions, are all the outcome of my experience. They have all been verified by years of experiment and observation.

For them I have no apologies to make. On the other hand, I am not a writer—I am a violinist. If, therefore, some apology is due my readers for the informality of my treatment of the subject, I can offer but one justification—that I have had but one purpose in the writing of this volume: to place at the disposal of teachers and students of the violin a brief, straightforward presentation of what it has taken me a lifetime to learn.

L. A.

INTRODUCTION

IN publishing this book on the art of violin playing, I should scarcely presume to lay claim to having made any novel discoveries with regard to the subject in question. I have merely endeavoured to present my own personal opinions—the fruit of my own experience as a violinist and a teacher of violin—in the hope of interesting those to whom the subject itself voices an appeal. Three great violin masters of the nineteenth century, Baillot, De Bériot and Spohr, were the first to set forth theoretically the principles underlying the art of violin playing. Various authorities of our own day have enlarged upon and developed these theories along the lines laid down by the masters of the past, and have, in addition, undertaken to demonstrate, in scientific fashion, the essentials of the more recent evolutions of their art. They have extended this theory of violin playing to include a careful analysis of the physical elements of the art, treating their subject from the *physical* point of view, and supporting their deductions by anatomical tables showing, to the very least detail, the structure of the hand and arm. And, by means of photographic reproductions, they have been able to show us the most authoritative poses, taken from life, to demonstrate how the bow should be held, which finger should press down the stick, how the left hand should be employed to hold the violin, and so on. What more could be done to guide the pupil and facilitate his task?

Yet the most essential factor, if the observance of these carefully formulated principles is to show any practical results, has hitherto been largely overlooked. This factor is the mental one. By no means enough stress has ever been laid on the importance of mental work, on the activity of the brain which must control that of the fingers. And yet, unless one is capable of hard mental labour and prolonged concentration, it is a waste of time to undertake the complicated task of mastering an instrument as difficult as the violin. It would seem then that—in view of the

many books dealing specifically with the violin and violin playing, a whole technical bibliography augmented by a rich collection of pictorial illustrations—all possibility of failure in this
particular direction might have disappeared. We are wont to take
for granted, even in observing a student who has received his
training at a school of no particular reputation, that he knows
how to handle the instrument satisfactorily, since, after all,
everything that can be said on that subject has been said over and
over again; all details of procedure have been minutely laid down,
and all that the conscientious student needs to do is to follow
them in order to attain perfection! Yet this entire body of
practical exposition has been productive of only meagre results.
The great majority of violin students—most of whom show but
slight interest in theoretical explanations—may be said to be
quite uneducated, violinistically speaking. And I know from my
own long years of experience as a violin teacher in Europe, and
more recently in America, that this is true.

One great mistake lies in the failure of so large a majority of
those who decide to devote themselves to music—to learning
some string instrument, the violin, for example—to ascertain
at the very outset whether nature has adequately supplied them
with the necessary tools for what they have in mind. They
apparently do not stop to consider that for a student to devote
himself to the mastery of the violin with no more than a vague
and uncertain idea of prerequisite conditions, is tantamount to
inviting failure. A keen sense of hearing is, above all, one of the
qualities which a musician needs. One who does not possess it in
the highest degree, is wasting his time when he centres his ambition on a musical career. Of course one may perfect one's
musical hearing if the faculty exists in even a rudimentary form
—though the student will have to be quick to improve it by
exact attention to the advice given him, and by unremitting
watchfulness while he is at work—but there must be a certain
amount of auditory sensibility to begin with. Then there is the
very important question of the physical conformation of the
hand, of the muscles, of the arm, of the wrist, of the elasticity
and power which the fingers possess. There are hands that
absolutely refuse to conform to technical requirements indispensable to mastery of the instrument. Many aspiring students

have hands, for instance, the fingers of which are too fat. (I have known students, however, who, despite this handicap, have through intelligent and assiduous practice managed to acquire a perfect intonation.) There are hands with fingers which are too flaccid, bending, which refuse to work at the very moment when they should be firmest. There are hands the fingers of which are so short that they can scarcely move within the limits of the first position where the distance between the intervals is greatest, and where they cannot possibly stretch octaves and tenths. And there are also weak fingers whose weakness inherently is so great that the very endeavour to strengthen them by exercise only increases their flaccidity.

But besides an adequate physical equipment, one of the qualifications most important to the musician is a sense of rhythm. Together with the sense of hearing, it is a *sine qua non* for everyone who wishes successfully to devote himself to music. The more conspicuously nature has gifted the young musical aspirant with a discriminating sense of hearing and a strong feeling for rhythm, the greater are his chances of reaching his goal. There is still, however, one more quality which the promising student must possess. It is what the French call *l'esprit de son métier*, the feeling of the professional man for the detail of his profession. He should have, by intuition—by instinct—the faculty of grasping all the technical fine points of his art, and an easy comprehension of all shades of musical meaning.

The parents of young children, or those who are in charge of their early training, so often fail to realize the seriousness of their act when they light-heartedly decide that a child shall have a musical career and forthwith select the instrument which is to bring him fame and wealth. (In the case of the poor, or those of slender means, the violin, as a rule, is the instrument favoured, because it may be bought so cheaply.) The fame of great artists of the present and of the past gives stimulus to their ambitions for the youngster, and refusing to be at all dissuaded by those who know by experience the hazards of such an undertaking, they cling determinedly to the cherished idea which has taken entire possession of them. So it is that parents strive persistently toward the goal they have arbitrarily set their child, without pausing to consider that they may possibly be sacrificing his whole future to their misguided ambition for him. They send the child to study with some celebrated teacher in Europe or at home —before the First World War Europe was preferred—to some teacher who has turned out famous artists—and wait expectantly for the realization of their hopes. They see no reason why their son or daughter should not one day soon gain as much fame and admiration as those others who have taken the world by storm. During the many years I have devoted to teaching the violin, I have had some characteristic examples of this attitude of mind. From far and near people came to get my opinion regarding the degree of talent shown by young aspirants to fame. In many cases, where it was plain that the lack of musical aptitude and inclination, or physical defects, disqualified the student, I was quite frank in saying so. In most cases those interested resented my decision and went off discontented, and hunted up other advisers who would look upon their pet scheme with more favour. As a matter of fact, however, I have only a few times in my whole experience been able to deter parents who cherished such an ambition for their child, or to save the young "virtuoso" from certain failure by inducing him to take up some other profession, in which he will stand a better chance of being useful to his fellow-beings, and at the same time gain a more assured means of support for himself.

The majority of those who wish to become musicians, in spite of the fact that they may possess unusual gifts, have no idea of the difficulties they will have to surmount, the moral tortures they will be called upon to endure, the disillusions they will experience, before they win recognition. Ambitious young musicians habitually fail to realize that it takes years and years of unremitting toil; that they must be well taught; that they must be well supplied with the tools of their craft; that they must have good health and great patience, in order to surmount the obstacles with which nature—and often man as well—will obstruct the road. They do not know that to genius alone the brilliant firmament of promise opens wide—and then only after long and arduous struggles. The history of music, and of the great musicians, offers endless examples to corroborate what I say.

VIOLIN PLAYING
As I Teach It

CHAPTER I

HOW I STUDIED THE VIOLIN

I FIRST began to play the violin when I was just a little over six years old. My teacher was the first violin of the small orchestra which on Sundays and festival days provided music for the Catholic church in the little town in Hungary where I was born. But this versatile teacher of mine did not confine himself to the violin: he gave piano lessons as well, and like most of his colleagues in those days, he combined the offices of organist and conductor, and while he was pedalling away with his feet, would direct with either hand, turn and turn about, while the other was playing on the manuals. Sixty or seventy years ago, we were far from having the wealth of teaching material at our disposal that we have in these days—especially in that little town in Hungary! There was no such thing, then, as a special method, nor special principles or systems of instruction. Every teacher taught as best he knew how, and without any supervision.

Since that time pedagogy in general has made tremendous progress, and the art of violin teaching has by no means lagged behind. Thanks now to special exercises devised for special purposes, scales, studies, *études* systematically and progressively arranged—so to speak—put up in tabloid form or by the ounce, like the medicines of the modern pharmacopoeia, this huge body of study material is easily accessible to the student youth of our own day. With such a wealth of material placed at his disposal, he cannot, if he is in any degree competent to take advantage of his opportunities, fail to profit thereby.

But of my own violin lessons almost seventy years ago I can remember little. I went to my teacher three or four times a week to take my lessons, but I no longer recall what the master had me play or how he taught me. But I kept on taking lessons from him for some two or three years until my parents—though they were very far from being wealthy, quite the contrary, in

1

fact!—decided, following the advice of friends, to send me to Budapest, the capital of Hungary, to enter the Conservatory of Music there.

My parents were acquainted with one of the violin professors at the Conservatory, Mr. Ridley Kohné, who had come from our home town, and was there regarded as one of its most famous men, because he had conquered a place for himself in the great city. At that time the great art of advertisement had not as yet been developed, and the reputation of an artist was established by tale and rumour, by the things which were said of him. Mr. Kohné, my future teacher, had by no means acquired a European reputation. He was well known only in his—and my own—natal town, and, to a lesser extent, in Budapest. But in that little village in Hungary where I lived, his standing—since he was a professor at the Conservatory in the greatest city in Hungary—was very high indeed.

When I reached Budapest, I was accepted at the Conservatory as a pupil, and at the same time placed in a boarding school, where it was arranged that I should take up my general studies. And in addition to studying regularly at the Conservatory, it was arranged that I should be given private lessons by my teacher.

I might remark that my teacher was *Concert meister* at the Budapest National Opera House, and that his companion among the first violins of the orchestra and also on the Conservatory staff, was the father of Jenö Hubay, the famous violinist-composer of today, who was at that time known by the name of Huber. I can remember that it was in Budapest that I first began to study systematically, along lines laid down in the *Ecole de Violon* by Alard, then professor at the Paris Conservatory.

In those days France dominated all Europe, musically speaking, and particularly Eastern Europe. Paris was the dream-vision that floated before the eyes of every young student, of every artist who yearned for recognition. But Paris seemed so far away, the dream of ever reaching it appeared so difficult of attainment! The actual physical process of getting to the city of our desires was anything but easy, owing to the lack of adequate railroads in Hungary. Yet every musician was drawn by all the magnetism of the imagination and all the powers of suggestion to that city on the Seine. Paris, the Paris Conservatory—that was our goal! The Conservatories of Vienna and Leipzig were scarcely known at the time, in spite of the real importance of both of them and of the Leipzig Conservatory especially.

In the conservatory at Budapest, however, I acquired a little technical facility, as the result of my study of Alard's *Ecole*, and I began to play little pieces within the compass of my ability— *études* by such composers as De Bériot and Artôt (the latter a Belgian violinist whose music was much affected by his contemporaries). I cannot recall having practised the Kreutzer and Rode *Etudes* while I was at Budapest, but I do recall having played the Rovelli *Etudes*.

I spent two years in the Hungarian capital, and then I was transferred to Vienna, to continue my studies in the home of Professor Jacques Dont, who, perhaps because his manner was so modest, was at that time not so very well known, in spite of his real genius as a teacher. It was due to M. Dont's rare skill as a teacher, and thanks to the interest he took in me, that I since really began to grasp and to understand the true character of the violin, and at the same time began to get some inkling of how very difficult it really is to master the instrument. It was Dont who laid the foundation for the technique which I acquired later on; for until I began to study with him I had been groping alone in darkness, feeling my way from one technical point to another. He guided me in my practice of his own preparatory studies for the Kreutzer and Rode *Etudes* (*Vorübungen zu den Kreutzer und Rode Etuden*), without allowing me to neglect the scales, and gradually introduced me to Dont's twenty-four *Caprices*, since used throughout the violinistic world, but at the time when I was learning to play them (between 1855–6) almost entirely unknown.

I also commenced to play some of the Spohr Concertos, and the same composer's Duos for two violins, which Professor Dont greatly admired. And it was Dont, also, who gave me my first piano lessons, and, in due course of time, while I was still living and working in his home, acquainted me with the Mozart piano sonatas and the Czerny *Etudes*.

Unfortunately, the state of my finances—or rather, those of my parents—made it impossible for me to continue my studies with this excellent teacher, this man who had shown me such

3

generous kindness, and who had taken such an interest in my career.

While living in Vienna, I had been encouraged by Professor Dont to attend the Vienna Conservatory, principally in order to continue my study of harmony, chamber-music and *ensemble* playing in the orchestra class, and I had occasionally attended the violin classes of Joseph Hellmesberger, a musician of the highest order, and a celebrated interpreter of string-quartet music. He was the first violin of an organization then widely known: the "Hellmesberger Quartet". Hellmesberger was also the conductor of the orchestra class, in whose work I was keenly interested, though I had not the slightest idea how to go about playing in an orchestra. Hence I was very much excited the first time I took part in one of its sessions. As I was in the conductor's own class in the Conservatory, I was given a place among the first violins, and when I had to attack the first measure—it was the *Egmont* overture, by Beethoven—I lost my head completely, owing to the unaccustomed burst of sonority from the instruments surrounding me. Nevertheless, I soon grew used to the *ensemble*, and in the course of time greatly enjoyed taking part in the orchestra work; while at the same time I laid a foundation for my knowledge of the orchestra. What I learned there in Vienna was of great service to me some forty years later in Petrograd, where I conducted the symphonic concerts of the "Imperial Russian Musical Society", founded by Anton Rubinstein—an organization which flourished up to the time of the Revolution of 1917.

It was in 1858 that I completed my course in Vienna and received the medal and diploma of the Conservatory, which later I found served me everywhere very acceptably as a passport in the provincial towns in which I played! But a career as a concert artist playing in small towns was by no means my dream! I played in them through force of circumstances, for my parents could no longer support me, and I had to gain my living as best I could, and whenever possible give such help as I could to my family who had done so much for me. I was only a young artist then, whose musical education was as yet uncompleted, handicapped at first by my lack of a sufficiently large and varied repertory. Little by little, however, I built up my repertory by using every opportunity that came to me to hear genuine virtuosos play while "on tour", and by hearing them play in Vienna, during my rare visits to that city—on which occasions I never failed to profit greatly by the advice of Professor Dont.

In those days there were comparatively few violinists travelling on concert tours. The means of transportation were inadequate, and travelling was anything but comfortable; hence the great artists of the time, men like Vieuxtemps, Bazzini, Laub, made but rare appearances. These three violinists, whom I was able to hear occasionally, made the greatest impression upon me, and I endeavoured to profit to the greatest possible degree by the example their playing set. Vieuxtemps impressed me particularly by the grandeur of his tone and the nobility of style displayed in his Concertos. Bazzini, a virtuoso in the true sense of the word, was distinguished by the singing quality of his tone, and the then altogether novel piquancies which he introduced in his compositions, and which made a veritable sensation in Vienna.

Every violinist of the day knew his scherzo *La Ronde des Lutins*, but few were acquainted with his fine *Allegro de Concert*. Considered as violin music, *Allegro de Concert* is a composition of really superior merit, well worth intensive study—which is sure to repay the student. Laub, as a violinist, shone by reason of his warmth and compactness of tone, and his perfect technique. I strove to perfect myself by observation of these models until that moment when, owing to a fortunate combination of circumstances, and being very warmly recommended to him, I went to Joachim, in Hanover, in 1862.

This was a milestone in my student life. Joachim was already celebrated in consequence of his affiliation with Liszt at Weimar, and, later, because of the fame he had acquired as a solo player in the great musical centres. He held an honorary position at the court of King George of Hanover, which was then an independent kingdom, later to be absorbed by the German Empire. King George was blind and a passionate lover of music. In order to induce Joachim to remain in his capital and make his permanent home there the King appointed him conductor of the Court Orchestra, to direct its symphonic concerts. Thus he secured an opportunity of hearing the master play for him frequently, in the most intimate way.

Besides myself there were half a dozen other young violinists whom the master had accepted as pupils. Our schedules were more than irregular! We had to be ready to take a lesson at any hour of the day that he came to town to teach us! His servant used to come to summon one or another of us. At the first lesson Joachim gave me I played Spohr's Eighth Concerto, the "Vocal Scene", for him, and I think my intonation was dubious; he told me as much, criticizing my style as well, and advising me to pay more careful attention to it. Then, in order to test me at the following lesson—our lesson-time was never fixed in advance—he gave me Rode's third *Etude*, in the second position, to prepare. We hardly ever played any scales or *études* for him during the lesson, with the single exception of some of the Paganini *Caprices*. Anything which had to do with the technique of the two hands we were supposed to attend to at home. Joachim very rarely entered into technical details, and never made suggestions to his pupils as to what they were to do to gain technical facility, how they were to carry out a certain bow-stroke, how a certain passage might best be played or how to facilitate its execution by using a given fingering. Throughout the lesson he kept his violin and bow in his hands, and whenever he was dissatisfied with the way the student played a passage or a musical phrase, the master would draw his bow and play the passage or phrase in question himself in a manner truly divine.

Besides the great classic works of violin literature, Joachim encouraged us to study the works of Ernst, whom he greatly admired, and whose compositions he encouraged his pupils to play for the sake of technical development. In this respect I follow Joachim's example. I advise my pupils to play a great deal of Ernst.

Whenever I had an opportunity of hearing Joachim play, I always felt as though he were a priest, thrilling his congregation with a sermon revealing the noblest moral beauties of a theme which could not help but interest all humanity. His playing, while one listened to it, revealed unsuspected horizons, but it would have been asking the impossible of him to have demanded that he be a teacher in the ordinary sense of the word. He rarely made his meaning clear in detail, and the only remark which he would utter at times, after having demonstrated a point, would

6

be: "*SO müssen Sie es spielen!*" (*That* is how you must play it!), accompanied by an encouraging smile.

Those among us who were able to understand him, who could follow his inarticulate indications, benefited enormously by them, and tried as far as possible to imitate him; the others, less fortunate, stood with wide-open mouth, uncomprehending, and fixed their attention on one or another of the great virtuoso's purely exterior habits of playing—and there they remained. My very fortunate experience as a pupil of Joachim's convinced me that the violin teacher should never confine his teaching to word of mouth. In spite of all verbal eloquence a teacher can call to his service, he will never be able to inculcate properly, to compel the pupil to grasp all the delicacies of execution, if he is unable to illustrate, by means of the violin itself, whatever he asks the pupil to do. Purely verbal teaching, teaching which only explains by means of the spoken word, is *dumb* teaching!

Of course the other extreme must be avoided also. Occasionally you find a teacher who for one reason or another considers it necessary to play in unison with his pupil throughout the lesson. I ask myself in vain: How is he going to follow his pupil's playing? and what results may be expected from instruction of this kind?

Of these two methods of teaching the first is, of course, to be preferred, even though it be not in accord with all that pedagogic principles demand, for at any rate it is not as disastrous in its effect upon the pupil as the second.

It was in the manner already described, then, that I went through the most important works of the violin repertory under the supervision of that great artist, Joachim—not, alas, without frequent interruptions in my lessons, owing to absences of my teacher on his concert tours! With him I studied the Beethoven and Mendelssohn Concertos (the Brahms Concerto had not as yet been written); Spohr; Bach's Sonatas for violin solo; Ernst's Concerto in F sharp minor, his *Airs hongrois*, "Otello" Fantasy, and *Rondeau Papageno*; and the famous Hungarian Concerto by Joachim himself, written as a tribute to his native land. This last is a work of the very first order, which every violinist of standing would do well to include in his repertory. This concerto is not as widely known and appreciated by violinists as it should be, in spite of its originality of character and a technical side which is quite out of the ordinary. Its second movement, especially—a "Pastorale" with variations—is a most poetic composition which, when played in a style in keeping with its character, as indicated by the composer, never fails to make a deep impression.

Joachim was incomparable in his knowledge of string-quartet literature, as well as of all chamber-music in general. In his home in Hanover he often played the choicest compositions of the classic repertory, with three excellent artists, members of the orchestra of the Royal Opera, for an intimate circle of friends. It was at these musicales that I became imbued with aspirations and ideals which I have treasured my whole life long; and it was at them that I for the first time heard a work by Brahms—the Sextet in G major—when the very fact of its composer's existence was as yet quite unknown to me. At these gatherings in the great violinist's home I met Ferdinand David and Johannes Brahms, then quite a young man, beardless, very shy, with long hair, and slenderly shaped. He seemed to me then more like a representative of Liszt's Weimarian school, and in no way seemed to suggest that he would later become a famous antagonist of that circle. I also made the acquaintance there of Mme Clara Schumann, Robert Schumann's widow, a highly esteemed pianist; Ferdinand Hiller, director of the Cologne Conservatory and conductor of the great Rhenan music festival, as well as a composer of distinction; Niels Gade, Denmark's greatest composer, and many others, a veritable host of artists who were passing through Hanover, or even going there especially to pay their respects to Joachim, as the greatest violinist-musician of his time.

So far as we, his pupils, were concerned, I have already indicated that each one of us had to deal with the technical side of his own problems as well as he knew how. For my part, I worked a great deal on simple scales and double-stops, and studied certain of the Kreutzer *Etudes*, especially the one in F major, in order to strengthen my third finger, which was naturally a little weak. Since there existed no special technical material for the left hand nor for the bow-arm, with the exception of the studies already mentioned, I invented some for myself; and, above all, I used passages from the different concertos and other pieces, passages of which I was not quite sure, as material for the extension and perfection of mechanism.

I recommend this last-mentioned procedure to students as a means whose good effect is certain. Such practice is of the greatest usefulness, since if one succeeds in this way in mastering one after another the passages which have hitherto seemed insurmountably difficult, a great step in advance in actual playing skill has necessarily been made. And besides that, the student has in the process gained self-confidence in his interpretation of the composition in question.

After two years (1863–5) spent in the delightful city of Hanover, I said farewell to Joachim, filled with gratitude for all he had done for me, and once more resumed my roaming musical life. From time to time I made my début in the celebrated concerts given at *Gewandhaus* in Leipzig (founded by Mendelssohn), and in other cities in Germany, Holland and the Scandinavian countries, and, finally, in London. I left that city in 1868, to accept the invitation extended to me to take the place of Henri Wieniawski at the Imperial Conservatory in Petrograd, Russia.

CHAPTER II

HOW TO HOLD THE VIOLIN

I

THE VIOLIN

IT is impossible to overestimate the importance of the first elementary practical steps in the long process of mastering the violin. For better or for worse, the habits formed in the early period of training directly influence the whole later development of the student. The very start of all violin playing—the apparently simple matter of holding the instrument, for instance, before the bow is brought into play at all—has a wide range of possibilities for good or for evil. There is no instrument whose absolute mastery at a later period presupposes such meticulous care and exactitude in the initial stages of study as does the violin. And, since holding the instrument as it should be held is prerequisite to all further development, this phase of violin teaching shall claim our first consideration.

In holding the violin the first thing to bear in mind is that it should be held in such a position that the eyes may be fixed on the head of the instrument, and the left arm should be thrust forward under the back of the violin so that the fingers will fall perpendicularly on the strings, the fingertips striking them with decided firmness.

The second important point is this: avoid resting the violin on the shoulder or, vice versa, shoving the shoulder *underneath the violin*. The placing of a cushion beneath the back of the instrument, in order to lend a more secure support to the chin grip, should also be avoided. These are bad habits, which one should from the very start carefully avoid, since they not only spoil the violinist's pose in general, but—and this is extremely important —*they make the player lose at least a third of the whole body of tone* which his violin—be it a fine or an indifferent instrument, a powerful or a weak one—is capable of producing.

As for the chin-rest, the one used should be adapted to the individual neck, so that by means of it the player is able to hold the instrument easily and without strain. Those violinists who rest the instrument against the shoulder, and place a cushion at its back—both of which act as mutes—evidently have no notion of the disastrous effect this arrangement has on their tone.

Always try to raise your violin as high as possible, in order to secure for your hand the greatest freedom of movement from one position to another. This may be accomplished by slightly advancing the left arm towards the chest.

Endeavour always to lessen the distance between the arms, to bring them together by inclining the body slightly to the left, yet without resting the left arm against the front of the body. At first you will not find it at all easy to raise the violin without support, but in the course of time one accustoms oneself to it, with a resultant gain in facility in reaching the higher positions, as well as in the playing of rapid descending passages.

If there be any question as to the advantage of holding the violin high, the student may draw his own conclusions by observing the leading exponents of his art. If we watch the great concert violinists of the day when they play in public, we shall discover that the majority of them hold their violins at a high level, especially when playing on the G-string, and thereby increase the vibrations of the instrument, and the string vibrations (not those produced by the hand) which represent the sound developed by the touch of the hair of the bow on the string.

II

THE POSITION OF THE THUMB

The thumb should not extend beyond the fingerboard of the instrument, since this prevents the player from using the G-string. Try to hold the thumb thrust forward more in the direction of the second and third fingers, so as to give the hand greater liberty of action by increasing its stretching powers.

In order to be certain that the hand is well placed, put it to this test: place the second finger on the note F, on the D-string, in the first position—if the thumb is directly opposite, on the self-same line, it is in the right place. To avoid an incorrect finger position in the first position (one of the most difficult so far as correct finger position is concerned), and at the same time to strengthen the fingers—and never forget that the fingers cannot be made too strong—place the four fingers on the four strings—the first on the F of the E-string; the second on the C of the A-string; the third on the G of the D-string; and the fourth on the D of the G-string. Do not raise any one of the fingers until all four are resting on the notes mentioned. When the fingers are all in place, exercise each finger separately, raising it and allowing it to drop back into place several times in succession. Begin with the second finger, then take the fourth, and then the first, and, finally, the third. The exercise should be carried out in such wise that the fingers not engaged remain on the strings. This exercise, persisted in, is certain to accomplish two valuable things—absolute correctness of finger position, especially as regards the thumb, and increased finger strength.

III

THE BOW

When I say that the hand should be lowered—or rather that the wrist should be allowed to drop when taking up the bow—and that as a consequence the fingers will fall into position on the stick naturally and of their own accord, I am expressing a personal opinion based on long experience. I myself have found that there can be no exact and unalterable rule laid down indicating which one or which ones of the fingers shall in one way or another grasp and press the stick in order to secure a certain effect. Pages upon pages have been written on this question without definitely answering it. I have found it a purely individual matter, based on physical and mental laws which it is impossible to analyse or explain mathematically. Only as the result of repeated experiment can the individual player hope to discover the best way in which to employ his fingers to obtain the desired effect.

HOW TO HOLD THE VIOLIN

Joachim, Wieniawski, Sarasate and others—every great violinist of the close of the last century—had each his own individual manner of holding the bow, since each one of them had a differently shaped and proportioned arm, muscles and fingers. Joachim, for instance, held his bow with his second, third and fourth fingers (I except the thumb), with his first finger often in the air. Ysaye, on the contrary, holds the bow with his first three fingers, with his little finger raised in the air. Sarasate used all his fingers on the stick, which did not prevent him from developing a free, singing tone and airy lightness in his passage-work. The single fact that can be positively established is that in producing their tone these great artists made exclusive use of *wrist-pressure* on the strings. (The arm must never be used for that purpose.) Yet which of the two, wrist-pressure or finger-pressure, these masters emphasized at a given moment—which they used when they wished to lend a certain definite colour to a phrase, or to throw into relief one or more notes which seemed worth while accenting—is a problem impossible of solution.

Incidentally, we may observe the same causes and the same effects in the bow technique of the virtuosi of the present time. They may have nothing in common either in talent or temperament, yet, notwithstanding this fact, each one of them will, according to his own individuality, produce a beautiful tone. The tone of the one may be more sonorous, that of the other more transparent, yet both will be ravishing to hear, and not even the closest attention will enable you to divine which form or degree of finger-pressure the artist has exerted to produce his tone. Young students cannot be told too often: "Sing, sing on your violin! It is the only way in which to make its voice tolerable to the listener."

CHAPTER III

HOW TO PRACTISE

Young students—in spite of all the advice lavished upon them—do not generally realize the importance which attaches to the manner in which they work, and the influence their mode of practising is bound to have upon their future.

Beyond question the student's progress depends very heavily upon his being properly guided and taught, and on his capacity—in keeping with whatever talent he may possess and whatever skill he may display—to profit by his teacher's advice. Yet the main essential is for him to cultivate the habit of close self-observation, and above all to accustom himself to direct and control his efforts. For it is this mental labour which is the true source of all progress.

The young student is prone to allow himself to be carried away by the impulse to execute a passage in a precipitate tempo, intoxicating himself with the sheer pleasure of his own digital velocity. This makes it impossible for him to follow each note with his ear, to hear the intonation of what he is playing. He cannot distinguish his imperfect intonation; he is unable to detect inequalities in the rapid flow of his passage-work; he does not know whether his tone production is good; whether each note is clearly enunciated; and whether or not there are any inequalities in his passages, due to the faulty movement of the fingers. The young violinist should be able to answer any of these questions, but, alas—owing to his habit of practising in too rapid a tempo—he is altogether at a loss where they are concerned. Yet let him remember that those who listen to him are able to hear and to judge impartially!

I thoroughly believe—and I always tell my pupils this—that when they practise without observing and criticizing themselves they merely develop and perfect their faults. They are worse than

14

wasting their time. I have had students, however, who in spite of good intention, became the victims of a nervous agitation the moment they took up their violins, and were wholly unable to resist the necessity of playing in an exaggeratedly rapid tempo. Such students were never born to become concert players. Among them are violinists who, though well endowed by nature, are subject to certain definite limitations. Once they have reached these limits which nature has set, no method, no amount of hard work will bring them any further. They stop short. Like a swimmer struggling against the current, they may dive headlong, pushing forward under water with all their might in an endeavour to make progress, only to find, on regaining the surface, that they have scarcely changed their position. The tide has been too strong for them. Players of this type make up the major portion of the army of the "unknown" or "unrecognized". If they are philosophical enough to accept a verdict of necessity and resign themselves to their limitations, they become excellent orchestra players. Many of them, also, devote themselves to teaching, often, however, without being very well adapted for the work.

The shape and conformation of the left hand are also responsible for the lack of success of a great number of students who seem otherwise well endowed. I have come across cases of this kind in Russia where young students coming from abroad, ill-advised by their teachers, practised from eight to ten hours a day in the vain hope of improving their technique and—because of this excess of uninterrupted labour—could scarcely move their fingers.

Yet even an expert cannot predict with certainty the skill which a particular hand may develop. It is as yet impossible for us to determine and establish with exactitude all the innumerable interrelations of the muscles and their reaction upon each other, nor the complexities of the action of the nerves of the fingers. How are we to explain the fact that two hands, belonging to two different human beings, which appear to be identical in size, with fingers which seem to be equally long and strong, nevertheless differ altogether in their action? Experience may show that the fingers of the one hand need to be kept continually active in order to retain their flexibility; while the fingers of the other may not be used for weeks at a time and yet, after some slight finger-gymnastic work and a small investment of time, regain all their agility and be ready to perform their functions perfectly. It is due to this apparently inexplicable fact that certain well-known virtuosos are obliged to practise continually in order to keep themselves in condition, while others may indulge in the luxury of allowing long periods of time to elapse in which they do not touch the instrument at all.

Sarasate once told me that he did not practise at all during the summer. Davidov, the greatest cellist of his time, who was director of the Petrograd Conservatory from 1880 to 1890 (where I myself was the head of the violin department) and with whom I played string quartet concerts for more than twenty years, always laid his Stradivarius away in the safe during the summer months. He did not take it out again until we were to meet for the first quartet rehearsal the following autumn, and he used no other instrument during the whole time which had intervened. Joachim, on the contrary, practised a great deal; and during his concert tours he played in the compartment of his railroad coach. Whether this was because he found it necessary to keep his fingers moving, or because he was nervous in general, I cannot say. It is a well-known fact that Joachim, when teaching, always had his Stradivarius in his hand, and illustrated practically all that he had to impart, playing himself, to the great benefit of those of his pupils who were able to profit by his great example.

As for myself, my hands are so weak and their conformation is so poor that when I have not played the violin for several successive days, and then take up the instrument, I feel as though I had altogether lost the faculty of playing. I cannot tell which of my two hands is more weakened by the period of inactivity, the left hand or the bow-arm hand.

But what I have meant to suggest here is that the great artists are exceptional. Each has his peculiarities, and one must not and should not try to imitate any one of them blindly. Rather you must try to catch the reflection of his genius and, utilizing whatever light it may shed, readapt it to your own individual needs. It is often the case, in fact, that when a great artist stresses some small defect or peculiarity in his playing, any number of young students will first of all seize upon the unessential personal quirk and believe that in so doing they have grasped the very essence

16

of the artist's genius. It is much easier to imitate, of course, this trifling defect than the more substantial qualities which, at bottom, make up the artist's true individuality.

But let us turn again from these more general considerations to the more specific matter of practice methods. In all practice-work, and this applies to the advanced student as well as the beginner, rest during practice hours should never be overlooked. My advice—based on the experience of years—is never to practise more than thirty or forty minutes in succession, and to rest and relax for at least ten or fifteen minutes before beginning work again. If this plan is carried out, and I should once more like to emphasize its value, the student, in order to practise from four to five hours a day must have, actually, six or seven hours at his disposal.

CHAPTER IV

TONE PRODUCTION

THE problem involved in the production of an entirely agreeable tone—that is to say a tone which is *singing* to a degree that leads the hearer to forget the physical process of its development—is one whose solution must always be the most important task of those who devote themselves to mastering the violin.

The question of tone production, we might as well acknowledge at once, is not primarily a matter of the hairs on the stick, of rosin, of change of bow on the strings, nor of change of position by means of the fingers of the left hand. All these really signify nothing, absolutely nothing, when it comes to the production of a pure crystalline and transparent violin tone. To obtain a tone of this quality, the student must not only expect to sacrifice whatever time may be necessary, but he must be willing to bring to bear on the problem all his intelligence, all the mental and spiritual concentration of which he is capable. And for guidance in this he must rely upon the precepts of the great masters of the past, and the example of the great violinists of the present day.

To describe in exact detail just how the bow should be held, just how the pressure of the fingers should be adjusted, and which finger—at a given moment—should stress its pressure upon the stick, and just how to set about beginning to use the wrist—*the central point round which everything relating to tone production turns*—all this presents a task of well-nigh insurmountable difficulty. But what holds good in the case of all other arts is true also of the violin. Natural instinct, physical predisposition, the construction of the muscles of the hands and of the bow-arm— each plays a determining part in the ultimate effect.

Clear and complete understanding, the gift of seizing and retaining the explanations of a good teacher, so far as my observation goes, is the only practical way of achieving the beautiful tone which should be the ambition of every violinist.

The value of the theories presented in instruction is doubled by the student's practical application of them; and the teacher's most important asset is a knowledge of how to employ the two means in conjunction and to make his theoretical teachings bear practical fruit. For the best of advice set down on paper, be it ever so useful, and based on the most valid scientific principles, can never take the place of the living, spoken word, followed by an actual demonstration of its application to the problem in hand.

Unfortunately, in no country in the world is musical instruction other than a free agent. Nowhere is it subjected to proper standards and adequate supervision. This is true even in those countries where the Government supports schools especially designed for the teaching of music, and so sets a high standard which private instruction seeks to approximate. But the private teacher everywhere is free from responsibility to his pupils; he can carry on his "business" in any fashion that pleases him. He sets his own standards and develops his own teaching methods— and there is no organization or system of inspection that requires that a teacher of the violin must have qualified for his work by a period of study at one of the great institutions. And in those countries, particularly, which have no State-supported or State-endowed schools of music, anyone who takes a fancy to give music-lessons may—if he can receive a few pupils—enter the profession! I do not by any means wish to imply that all private teachers are irresponsible. Many are indeed desirous of doing their best, but alas, having themselves been ill-taught, they spread the poison of their own ignorance broadcast, a plague which carries off many hapless innocents, victims of their pernicious teaching methods.

I stress the importance of competent teaching in connexion with the subject of tone production because the acquisition of a pure, lovely tone is emphatically a matter of instructive development, and it is so largely within the power of the teacher to foster or destroy its latent possibilities in his pupils, that he is anything but a negligible factor in its attainment. More national conservatories, the faculties of whose violin departments would be made up of the best teachers obtainable, and the compulsory standardization of private violin instruction, would improve the tone production of violin students the world over.

Returning to the detailed consideration of our subject, I shall here outline—in a form best suited for the student's practical application of the advice—what my own teaching experience has demonstrated in the matter of tone production.

SOME HINTS ON THE SUBJECT OF TONE PRODUCTION

I

When taking up the bow with the fingers, lower the hand in such a way that the bow falls naturally into position, of its own accord. By so doing you will obviate the feeling which impels you to cling tightly to the stick.

II

Hold the bow lightly, yet with sufficient firmness to be able to handle it with ease; above all, do not try to bring out a big tone by pressing the bow on the strings. This is an art in itself, and can only be developed by means of hard work and experience.

III

Do not press down the bow with the arm: *the whole body of sound* should be produced by means of a light pressure of the wrist, which may be increased, little by little, until it calls forth a full tone, perfectly pure and equal in power, from the nut to the point of the bow, and vice versa.

IV

Begin with slow strokes with the whole length of the bow, allowing ten or twelve seconds for each down- and up-stroke, and stop as soon as you feel fatigue. The muscles and the joints of the wrist and forearm stand in need of relaxation after an effort which, however slight, has been continuous.

TONE PRODUCTION

V

The degree of finger-pressure to be applied to the stick is a question of experience, of observation from the instructive side, and also of discipline.

VI

In order to learn properly how to obtain an equal tone, both at the nut and at the point of the bow, the natural tendency of the hand to press down upon the bow at the nut—because of the greater weight of this part of the stick—and, contrariwise, to weaken at the point—the weakest portion of the stick—must be counterbalanced by additional pressure—always of the wrist.

VII

Play as slowly as possible the sustained notes of a scale, in the following manner:

and so forth, first through two octaves and later, when you feel greater confidence, to the third-octave G, taking care, while increasing the tone, to augment it only by finger-pressure, not by arm-pressure, thus avoiding forcing the tone which otherwise grows rough. Transpose as you may see fit. Once the habit of drawing a pure, colourful tone from the strings has been established, you may pass to sustained double-stops, to be played in accordance with the principles already laid down.

VIII

Play between the bridge and the fingerboard, for it is within this compass that the tone is most full and sonorous. Only when it is desirable to secure a very soft, sweet tone, *pp*, may you play near the fingerboard and even *upon* it. On the other hand, as soon as you play near the bridge with any degree of strength the tone grows harsh. When playing absolutely *pp*, no more than brushing the strings, the effect known as the *flautato*, which imitates the timbre of the flute-tone, is obtained. In each and every stroke, the bow should move in a straight line running parallel with the bridge.

IX

THE *VIBRATO*

The purpose of the *vibrato*, the wavering effect of tone secured by rapid oscillation of a finger on the string which it stops, is to lend more expressive quality to a musical phrase, and even to a single note of a phrase. Like the *portamento*, the *vibrato* is primarily a means used to heighten effect, to embellish and beautify a singing passage or tone. Unfortunately, both singers and players of string instruments frequently abuse this effect just as they do the *portamento*, and by so doing they have called into being a plague of the most inartistic nature, one to which ninety out of every hundred vocal and instrumental soloists fall victim.

Some of the performers who habitually make use of the *vibrato* are under the impression that they are making their playing more effective, and some of them find the *vibrato* a very convenient device for hiding bad intonation or bad tone production. But such an artifice is worse than useless. That student is wise who listens intelligently to his own playing, admits to himself that his intonation or tone production is bad, and then undertakes to improve it. Resorting to the *vibrato* in an ostrich-like endeavour to conceal bad tone production and intonation from oneself and from others not only halts progress in the improvement of one's fault, but is out and out dishonest artistically.

But the other class of violinists who habitually make use of the device—those who are convinced that an eternal *vibrato* is the secret of soulful playing, of piquancy in performance—are pitifully misguided in their belief. In some cases, no doubt, they are, perhaps against their own better instincts, conscientiously carrying out the instructions of unmusical teachers. But their own appreciation of musical values ought to tell them how false is the notion that vibration, whether in good or bad taste, adds spice and flavour to their playing. If they attempted to eat a meal in which the soup were too salt, the entrée deluged with a garlic-sauce, the roast too highly peppered with cayenne, the salad-dressing all mustard, and the dessert over-sweet, their palates would not fail to let them know that the entire dinner was over-spiced. But their musical taste (or what does service for them in place of it) does not tell them that they can reduce a programme of the most dissimilar pieces to the same dead level of monotony by peppering them all with the tabasco of a continuous *vibrato*. No, the *vibrato* is an effect, an embellishment; it can lend a touch of divine pathos to the climax of a phrase or the course of a passage, but only if the player has cultivated a delicate sense of proportion in the use of it.

With certain violinists, this undue and painful *vibrato* is represented by a slow and continuous oscillation of the entire hand, and sometimes by a precipitate oscillation of the hand and all the fingers as well, even those fingers which may be unoccupied for the time being. But this curious habit of oscillating and vibrating on each and every tone amounts to an actual *physical* defect, whose existence those who are cursed with it do not in most cases even suspect. The source of this physical evil generally may be traced to a group of sick or ailing nerves, hitherto undiscovered. And this belief of mine is based on the fact that I cannot otherwise account for certain pupils of mine, who in spite of their earnest determination to the contrary, and innumerable corrections on my part, have been unable to rid themselves of this vicious habit, and have continued to vibrate on every note, long or short, playing even the driest scale passages and exercises in constant *vibrato*.

There is only one remedy which may be depended upon to counteract this ailing nervous condition, vicious habit, or lack of good taste—and that is to deny oneself the use of the *vibrato* altogether. Observe and follow your playing with all the mental concentration at your disposal. As soon as you notice the slightest vibration of hand or finger, stop playing, rest for a few minutes, and then begin once more, continuing to observe yourself. For weeks and months you must continually guard yourself in this fashion until you are confident that you have mastered your *vibrato* absolutely, that it is entirely within your control. You may then put it to proper artistic use, as your servant, not your master.

In any case, remember that only the most sparing use of the *vibrato* is desirable; the too generous employment of the device defeats the purpose for which you use it. The excessive *vibrato* is a habit for which I have no tolerance, and I always fight against it when I observe it in my pupils—though often, I must admit, without success. As a rule I forbid my students using the *vibrato* at all on notes which are not sustained, and I earnestly advise them not to abuse it even in the case of sustained notes which succeed each other in a phrase.

THE *PORTAMENTO* OR *GLISSANDO*

The connecting of two tones distant one from the other, whether produced on the same or on different strings, is, when used in moderation and with good taste, one of the great violin effects, which lends animation and expression to singing phrases.

But the *portamento* becomes objectionable and inartistic— resembling more than anything else, it seems to me, the mewing of a cat—when it is executed in a languishing manner, and used continually. The *portamento* should be employed only when the melody is descending, save for certain very exceptional cases of ascending melody. In order to develop your judgment as to the proper and improper use of the *portamento*, observe the manner in which it is used by good singers and by poor ones. The violinist who is tempted to make careless use of the *portamento* will find that it is the easiest thing in the world to turn this simplest of expressive means into caricature merely by dragging the finger slowly from one tone to another, allowing the whole scale to be heard between the two objective points. For the sensitive ear this is nothing short of torture, though, alas, it is a form of cruelty only too often practised on the concert platform and in the "studio"

Like the *vibrato*, the *portamento* or *glissando* is one of the most telling of violin effects—if it is used with restraint, in a proper way, at the proper time. The violinist must always remember that the *glissando* is effective in proportion to the infrequency with which it is used. This may sound paradoxical, but is true. Only on occasion does it produce a beautiful effect. One means to which the string player may resort in order to determine whether or no he will do well to employ the *portamento* in a particular passage, is to sing the descending phrase or phrases to himself, and trust his ear to tell him whether or not the effect has justification, musically.

For me all those violinists who abuse the *effects* of violin playing, who are obsessed with the idea that the spicing of the tone they produce with *vibrato, portamento* and other similar devices is more important than the tone itself, belong in the second of the three classes into which the violinist Salomon divided all players of the instrument. King George III, to whom Salomon was giving violin lessons, asked his teacher to tell him how he was getting along. "Well," said Salomon to his illustrious pupil, "all violin players may be divided into three classes. The first class includes all those who cannot play at all; the second class those who play very badly; and the third class those who play well. Your Majesty has already managed to advance to the second class."

CHAPTER V

HINTS ON BOWING

I

THE *DETACHE* (DETACHED STROKE)

THE *détaché*, together with the "spun" or sustained tones —*sons filés* the French call them—which we have described in the preceding chapter, forms the foundation of all bowing technique.

In playing the detached stroke use the whole length of the bow, playing in a moderate tempo, and endeavour to secure a tone of equalized strength in the up- and down-strokes. Always attack each stroke from the wrist, continuing as the forearm enters into play, until you reach either the point at the down-stroke, or the nut, at the up-stroke. Vary this stroke by using different sections of the bow separately playing with the upper bow, in the middle, and at the nut.

II

THE *MARTELE* (HAMMER-STROKE)

This stroke, which is made at the point of the bow, is in itself very essential, and its use presents the additional physical advantage of reinforcing the muscles of the wrist. It is the basis of two other forms of the stroke: the *staccato* and the "dotted note" strokes which, like the *martelé*, are played at the point of the bow.

The *martelé* is obtained by pressing the string down firmly with the point of the bow, and making use of the wrist exclusively to produce the tone desired. In case you find yourself unable to master this stroke by use of the wrist alone, you may have recourse to a slight pressure of the forearm, but *never* to an upper arm or shoulder pressure.

III

THE *STACCATO* UP-AND-DOWN BOW

Opinions differ as to the manner in which the *staccato* stroke should be delivered. The masters of the past century, Kreutzer, Rode, Spohr and others, taught that the *staccato* stroke should be produced with the aid of the wrist. Spohr must have had an admirable *staccato*; he has indicated its use in his concertos to a considerable extent. Some of the great virtuosi of the nineteenth century whom I myself have heard play—Joachim for instance, whose pupil I have the honour to be—had only a moderately rapid *staccato*. Joachim produced his *staccato* only from the wrist, and it was just rapid enough for the demands of the classical repertory which he preferred in his concerts and his chamber-music performances. (Joachim was, by the way, the first to cultivate the principle: "The virtuoso exists for music, not music for the virtuoso." He it was who first popularized the Beethoven Violin Concerto, Bach's solo violin sonatas, and, above all, his "Chaconne", Tartini's Sonatas, particularly the one known as "The Devil's Trill", and a large portion of the classical repertory which figures on the concert-programmes of our own day.)

In my youth I heard Vieuxtemps play his concertos and some other of his own compositions. He produced his *staccati* in a mixed manner, from the wrist and from the forearm, and was able to play a great number of notes on the same bow-stroke, thus securing the most astonishing effects.

Wieniawski, however, was decidedly the most brilliant exponent of the *staccato* stroke. He used the *upper arm* only, stiffening the wrist to a point of actual inflexibility. His *staccati* were dizzingly rapid and at the same time possessed a mechanical equality. This method of production I myself have discovered to be the most efficacious. I use it.

Sarasate, on the contrary, who had a dazzling tone, merely used the *staccato volant*, the "flying" *staccato*, not too fast a type, yet one infinitely graceful. This last quality, grace, illumined all his playing, and was sustained by a tone of a supreme singing quality which, however, was not very powerful.

IV

THE *STACCATO VOLANT* ("FLYING *STACCATO*")

The *Staccato volant* ("Flying *Staccato*") is a combination of the two methods—playing from the upper arm, as well as from the wrist, using both at the same time, with the difference—that in the firm *staccato*, the bow does not leave the string, but sticks to it, so to speak, while in the flying *staccato* the bow is raised in an elastic manner after each note.

Here again, only visual demonstration of the methods of playing the *staccato* is of actual service to the student. But on the ground of long experience, I must admit that something besides proper instruction in playing the *staccato* is necessary to success. The student must have in addition a certain natural predisposition to the stroke, and his wrist must be capable of functioning as though impelled by a spring of the finest steel.

V

THE *SPICCATO SAUTILLE*
(*SPICCATO* WITH BOUNCING, SPRINGING BOW)

I have always taught the *spiccato* with bouncing, springing bow by means of a very slight *détaché* in the middle of the bow, played as short as possible, without any effort and making use of the wrist only; and above all, playing at a moderate tempo. In practising this bowing, the speed at which it is played may be gradually increased, the bow staying well on the string. After the wrist has gained a certain amount of agility, exercises on two strings (G-D) may be begun. And then the same exercise may be

carried out on the remaining two strings (A-E). In order to secure the *spiccato*, all that is necessary is to relax the pressure of the fingers on the bow, while going on with the same movement of the wrist used for the short detached stroke already mentioned. The bow will bound of its own accord if violent movements of the hand are avoided.

Excess in this direction, the endeavour to make the bow bound as much as possible by main strength, has an altogether contrary effect. The stick makes irregular bounds and leaps, and you will find yourself unable to control and master it. In order to give greater body to the tone all you need do is—without changing the position of the wrist—to hold the bow in such a way as to be able to use three-quarters of the breadth of the bow hairs. The hand should remain quiet, and keep to its usual position. The third finger only should execute an almost invisible movement, turning the bow in such a way that more hairs are brought to bear on the strings, since otherwise the tone will be feeble, without resonance, and the few hairs which touch the string will go sliding from one spot to another with a whistling tone. And you must try to keep the bow in the same place, between bridge and finger-board, in order that this whistling may be avoided.

VI

THE *RICOCHET-SALTATO*
(REBOUND WITH SPRINGING BOW)

For this bowing the bow should be held as lightly as possible, the fingers hardly touching the stick. The bow should be raised a quarter of an inch or more above the strings (depending on the weight and the elasticity of the stick as much as on the skill with which the movement is executed). Let it fall with an elastic movement of the wrist, and you will find that it will rebound as far as you freely allow it to. At first you will find that this gives you a certain number of unequally hurried tones. But after working for a time along the lines laid down you will succeed in guiding this irregular movement and will be able to play two, three, six and eight notes in an absolutely rhythmic manner with one bow-stroke, according as you may shorten or lengthen it.

29

THE *TREMOLO*

Two bow-strokes, delivered in close proximity, and in accordance with the same principles by which the *ricochet-saltato* stroke just considered is produced, should be employed for the *tremolo*. Give each down-bow a clearly marked accent from the wrist, which should be greatly relaxed in order to make the bow rebound. The more relaxed and elastic the accent the more the bow will leap. This applies also to the rebound in the case of the up-bow.

De Bériot has employed this bowing in a brilliant composition entitled "Le Tremolo", a variation on the Andante from the Sonata in A major, Op. 47—which, being dedicated to Kreutzer, is known as the "Kreutzer Sonata"—by Beethoven. François Prume, a virtuoso highly appreciated during the middle of the last century, also made extensive use of the *tremolo* in a number which became extremely popular, "La Mélancholie".

Quite recently Henri Marteau (who was professor of violin at the Berlin *Hochschule* from Joachim's death until the outbreak of the Great War) has used the *tremolo*—which had for a number of years been neglected by virtuosi and the composers—in several of his pieces.

VIII

THE ARPEGGIO

Like the *tremolo*, the arpeggio is produced in accordance with the principles by which the *ricochet-saltato* is delivered. If you wish to facilitate your arpeggio-work you must begin to study it *legato* in order to accustom yourself to passing over the four strings with an equalized movement of down-bow and up-bow. This you do without any forcing of the hand, employing the upper half of the bow. In order to secure a better attack on the G-string, you must raise your arm slightly and lower it so far as may be necessary in order to touch the two strings, A and E, with ease. Once you are quite sure of this movement, you may attempt to play the arpeggio as you would the *tremolo*, attacking it with an elastic wrist-stroke in the down-bow in order to make it "come off" as it should.

IX

THE *LEGATO*

The *legato* bowing is one of the strokes most used, and when perfectly played has a quality of great charm. In order to develop it properly, pass from one string to another by means of the wrist, supported by the forearm if you wish to attack; or pass to the A-string or E-string, the G-string and D-string, and back again to the A and E, letting the arm resume its customary position. But this movement of the arm as it passes over the various strings must be made in an almost imperceptible manner, without any trace of brusqueness. In perfecting your *legato* bowing in the manner I have here indicated you will find that in the course of time you will be able to play a large number of notes on one stroke. It is of advantage to practise this stroke in different keys and in different intervals, such as thirds, sixths and octaves, at first in quarter-notes, very slowly, then in eighths and six-teenths. Then change strings: move to the A- and the E-string.

Slowly

Place your bow on the two strings G-D, *or* on the two strings A-E, and sound the tone produced by the bow without pressure, without attempting to increase or diminish it. After a period devoted to the intelligent practice of the exercises already indicated, you may proceed to the special, easy studies of Kayser, Fiorillo, and to those of Kreutzer, using for these last the edition revised by Mazas. Alexander Bloch's *Principles and Practice of Violin Bowing* will be an invaluable aid, especially in the case of beginners. Transpose this exercise into various keys; use other intervals: thirds, sixths, octaves. Somewhat later try to play eighths and sixteenths—in one bow increasing the number of notes played on one and the same bow, and the tempo as well in proportion to the increase in the student's agility in moving across the strings, and from one position to another.

In order to secure a really perfect *legato*, the fingers which rest on the two strings must keep their place while the bow moves from one to the other. By raising either of the fingers the continuity of the tone is broken, and a species of stuttering is evident in the tone production.

Legato is really the negation of angles in violin playing. It is the realizing of an ideal—the ideal of a smooth, round, continuous flow of tone. *Legato* bowing, if developed as I have suggested, gives us the beautiful singing tone which is the normal tone of the instrument. Of course we must employ the *détaché*, the *martelé*, the *staccato* and other strokes—for the beauty of the sustained tone, the *son filé*, has to be brought out, it has to be shown in relief lest its very perfection grow monotonous. Yet the *legato* is the essence of all *cantabile* playing—you cannot sing on the violin without it. And even when it is only slightly relieved, it doesn't, in many instances, make a monotonous impression. To borrow an example from the literature of song, take some of the long *arias* in Bach's little cantatas. They are as a rule preceded by a recitative. But Bach, that great master, knew that nothing wearies the musical ear more quickly than extended recitative passages in a declamatory style, in a kind of vocal *détaché*—so he wrote short recitatives, while his arias were long.

But in these modern days—in orchestral music and in choral music particularly—the true *legato*, which is the means of expressing melody, has suffered an eclipse. There is so much of the intellect, of the mind, in modern musical development that melody, genuine melody, has suffered, and its medium of expression, the vocal or instrumental *legato*, has been thrust into the background.

This is in no sense true, however, in the case of violin music. For the violin is still a homophone instrument, a melody instrument, a singing instrument. Its chief beauty in expression is still the *cantabile* melody line. All the triumphs of virtuosity—the conquest of the double-trill, of the perfected *staccato* strokes, of fingered octaves and of tenths cannot change that fundamental fact. And that is why the *legato* bow-stroke, which is the melody-producing stroke, will continue to be one of the strokes most used, the stroke of them all which every violinist must develop in a really perfect manner if his string-song is to be unbroken and his tone production equalized and connected. And upon the mind of every violinist who desires to acquire a good *legato* bowing I should like to impress the following general rule:

Do not raise the finger on one string before the tone of the next string sounds.

CHAPTER VI

LEFT-HAND TECHNIQUE

SINCE playing in one position only is so elemental a matter as scarcely to justify the use of the word "technique" in its more comprehensive sense, a consideration of left-hand technique would of necessity begin with the change of positions. Then I wish to say something of the pressure of the fingers on the strings, and to make some suggestions concerning scales, and other exercises and fingering.

THE CHANGE OF POSITIONS

In passing from one position to another, the violin student should take particular pains to see that this change—or rather this transition from one position to another, beginning from the first—is effected in an *inaudible* manner. This is the first essential. In playing the scale on the E-string, for instance, the first finger, in shifting to the third position, must do so without the slightest *glissando* being audible. Though the first finger rests firmly on the string, nevertheless it must never press down in such a way that it cannot advance easily into the next position desired. And similarly, when descending into the first position, the first finger does not leave the string during this movement, but remains firmly in place, while the second finger, held as close as possible to the first, is ready to take its place in the first position with a movement so precipitate as to avoid making a *glissando*. The transition should be effected in a manner as completely inaudible and unnoticeable as is the legato movement from note to note in the following scale on the piano:

LEFT-HAND TECHNIQUE

This same rule should be observed when you wish to ascend or descend by the second and third fingers, and on the three remaining strings, the rule remains the same, irrespective of the fingering used.

If you neglect to follow this rule, or fail to pay sufficient attention to it, you may be sure that your carelessness is certain to spoil a "singing" phrase as well as a brilliant passage. Even though your intonation be good, and your tone agreeable, the effect of an inept change of position is always disastrous.

The thumb, however, plays no very important part in the shift or passage from one position to another. Attention should be paid, nevertheless, to the following details: the thumb should not cling tightly to the neck of the instrument in the first position; and it should not clutch hold of the fingerboard—which so often happens in the case of beginners. Let the thumb rest lightly against the neck of the instrument and follow after the first finger in moving into the various positions, thus aiding the hand to ascend and descend, without clinging or sticking, unless it be in passing into the higher positions, the fifth, sixth, seventh, etc. In such cases the thumb must be held in the middle, towards the end of the neck near the ribs, aiding the hand in its descent by withdrawing little by little.

Altogether too much is made of the thumb's importance, it seems to me. So often pupils coming to me from abroad ask me how to handle the thumb. I always tell them not to think about it too much, and give them the rules I have just laid down. I always point out that the first duty of the thumb is to hold the violin in the hollow between the thumb and first finger, so that the instrument will not drop out of the player's hand. This, in my opinion, is its primary function, and after that come the other functions I have already described.

THE PRESSURE OF THE FINGERS ON THE STRINGS

The question of finger-pressure is one of those widely discussed matters regarding which diametrically opposing opinions exist. The masters of the past century issued no edicts on the subject, leaving its decision partly to the individual teacher, and partly to the student's own instinct. The teacher was supposed to decide from observation of his pupil's fingers and hand, what degree of pressure was desirable in a particular case, and to advise the use of a stronger or weaker finger-pressure on the strings, in proportion to the student's actual physical strength. The teacher was also supposed to take into consideration the shape of the pupil's hand, and the pupil's own instinct would lead him to observe the difference in his tone production which resulted from a more or less powerful finger-pressure.

And the older masters were right in not making any hard and fixed rules regarding the matter, for such rulings have always to be changed in the case of each individual player. There are fingers built like steel which, falling on the strings, exert, without the least effort, a pressure sufficiently strong to call forth the vibration necessary when the bow attacks them. Other fingers, less favoured by fortune, have to press down more strongly to secure the same effect.

Since no two players have the same characteristics—and this holds good for their hands and fingers as well—it is obviously unwise to try to lay down rules governing the point at issue.

There are those who in specific monographs have advised "relaxation" *of the hand* on every occasion! Well, I myself believe in relaxation, when the word denotes general repose when working, or is employed as a synonym for a certain elasticity of the bow-arm, freedom of the wrist, and light pressure of the fingers on the stick. But, if we are speaking of "relaxation" of the left hand, that is to say, of the fingers of the left hand, then I am of the contrary opinion.

In fact, I believe so strongly that this is a false conception, that I feel I must insist that *the pressure of the fingers must conform in exact measure to their physical strength*. I will even go so far as to say that the more one tries to diminish the body of tone, in a *piano* and *pianissimo*, for instance, the more one should

36

increase the finger pressure, especially in the positions where the strings are raised higher above the fingerboard, and in the acute notes on the E-string rising from:

The greater the finger pressure you exert in this region of the fingerboard, the more rapidly these notes will vibrate beneath a slight pressure of the bow. On the other hand, the more you force the tone of these high, shrill notes, the more unpleasantly they affect the ear, since you cut the limited vibration by leaving too short a space between finger and bridge.

SCALES AND OTHER EXERCISES

There is just one and only one efficacious means of acquiring the technique indispensable to the left hand, that will supply the necessary independence, strength and agility, the training which the fingers must have. This means consists of the scales and special exercises, and all who desire to attain to any degree of perfection in violin-playing must undergo this discipline in order to reach their goal. Some may devote more and others less time to it, depending on physical and psychic conditions, but everyone must get his training sooner or later this way.

To attain even a limited degree of perfection—and perfection in art is limitless—the hand of a violinist must not only be physically adapted to the purpose, but its owner must be ambitious and patient, and capable of working hard and continuously. It is a long and arduous road, and even more arid and discouraging for such violinists-to-be as have not laid the foundation of their art at an age when most children are playing about with their comrades in the streets and on the greens of the public parks. Geniuses or great talents rarely have an opportunity to enjoy the pleasures of childhood when they are children!

In the case of the violinist, the sooner serious study begins the better. It is in early youth, from the age of six or seven on, while the muscles still have a certain softness and, at the same time, a certain elasticity, that they may best be shaped and trained for the great task they are set to accomplish—the development of a perfect technique. And even in these earliest years, the child must be guided in his work by a conscientious and experienced teacher. It is a great mistake to believe that any chance teacher will answer for the task, and that the cheapest violin is just about good enough for a beginning student. One must not forget that even the most gifted child will feel repulsion and discouragement if he has to listen to the harsh disagreeable tone of a cheap violin, particularly during his first lessons when, utterly unskilled in holding the bow, and ignorant of how to adjust it to the strings, he draws it this way and that, failing to hold it in vertical line with the bridge.

The history of music and the biographies of the great violinists indicate that the majority of them began their studies at an age varying from five to seven years. I know personally that Joachim, Wieniawski, Sarasate, Wilhelmj, and more recently Elman, Zimbalist, Heifetz, Toscha Seidel, Kathleen Parlow, Eddy Brown, Michel Piastro, Max Rosen and other artists now playing in public, began their violin practice at this age—when other children of equal years are still playing with their toys.

I stress this whole matter of the sacrifices which the beginner must make for his art's sake in connection with the study of scales and special exercises, because this indispensable and not too attractive means to perfection is one to which the student must of necessity devote himself in the earliest stages of his work. What, then, is the first step in learning to play a scale? First play the scale in the compass of *one* octave only, paying the greatest attention to your intonation. If your teacher is really conscientious, he will not pass over a single false note, and you will thus become accustomed from the very start to watch yourself while you are working with him.

The best "natural good ear" may become corrupted by negligence, and faulty intonation in the case of the half-steps—a very prevalent vice—is a menace against which you must especially be on your guard. If the half-steps are not sufficiently near each other, their intonation will always be dubious. Neglect of the half-tone progressions is at the very root of poor intonation—which does not mean, of course, the correct intonation of the whole tones is not to be just as carefully cultivated. For distances between the intervals, already very slight in the first four positions, become impossible of measurement—even with the aid of a magnifying glass—in the positions above the fourth. Therefore try to secure from the very beginning the most perfect intonation of whole tone and half-tone progressions.

After having gone over several scales in the major and minor keys in the compass of one octave, you may then take up a scale and play it through two octaves, always slowly, and using first the detached stroke and then the *legato* stroke; first playing four notes to each bow, then eight and, later, as many notes as you can execute evenly and with a fine, sonorous tone.

The teacher will do well to vary these scale exercises with short pieces of an easy, singable character, accompanied by a second violin or by the piano. This will increase the student's enthusiasm for his instrument and his studies, and will at the same time develop his ear, his good taste and his musical sensibility.

There is a considerable range of teaching material which may properly be used. One may begin with the scales as arranged by Ernest Lent. *Scales and Chord Studies for Violin*, a compilation by William F. Happich, contain valuable theoretical and historical indications regarding the music of the ancients. Schradieck's *Scales*, and the first book of his *School of Technique* for violin, contain exercises for the development of the left hand.

CHROMATIC SCALES

The practice of chromatic scales is too generally neglected by violin students, in spite of the fact that these scales are very often encountered later in concert pieces. It is of real importance that chromatic scales be played with skill and precision and, especially, that the student know thoroughly well how to form them, so that each note stands out clearly, lest the whole series be mistaken for some variety of caterwauling. This point cannot be stressed too much.

The basis of the chromatic scales is the half-tone movement

which, whether the progression be upward or downard, should be carried out rapidly—not rapidly in the musical sense of the word, as a tempo, but rapidly in the sense of physical motion. This quickness of physical movement on the part of the fingers should be developed without reference to the musical tempi, which may be taken as slowly as desired. This is the very first rule in studying chromatic scales.

The second rule is that, when changing from one string to another in the descending scale, all four fingers drop into place at one and the same time. As a result of this, sliding for more than a half-tone becomes a practical impossibility; the scale is produced in a clear and even manner and, above all, the caterwauling effect already alluded to is obviated.

The chromatic scales should also be practised in the various positions. These scales produce a very pleasing effect when enunciated with the same clarity as on the piano, and are exceedingly attractive and effective when they occur, for instance, as they do in the Spohr Concertos. Aside from their musical value, they supply an excellent exercise for strengthening the fingers and increasing their powers of resistance.

A wealth of material for the study of the chromatic scales will be found in the *Scale and Chord Studies for Violin* by William F. Happich, recommended above. The same book contains also arpeggio exercises in all the major and minor keys, the use of which I earnestly advise as a means of extending and fortifying the student's technique. Nor should the young violinist forget to practise the arpeggio on the chord of the seventh, and that on the chord of the ninth in the same volume, since both are excellent for perfecting intonation.

FINGERING

Fingering is primarily an individual matter; the conformation of the hand, the structure and the strength of the fingers determine whether one or another fingering is easier or more difficult for a particular student. A fingering which may be easy for one hand, may be quite inconvenient for another. For this reason those who revise and edit instructive violin works ought always to ask themselves whether their hands are of normal size—

neither unduly large nor very small—and then plan and indicate their fingerings from the point of view of what the normally shaped hand can most successfully accomplish. As to abnormal hands, they will always find a way of adapting themselves to the fingerings which they alone can use.

In general the student will be wise to allow himself to be guided, principally, by "rhythmic fingering", that is, to effect changes of position as indicated by means of rhythmic instinct. For instance:

and not

and again:

and not

Students and young artists will do well to guard against the antirhythmic fingerings shown in the preceding examples, through whose use the meaning and character of a musical phrase may easily be destroyed.

41

VIOLIN PLAYING AS I TEACH IT

The ability a beginning student displays, the progress he makes, and in a still greater degree the teacher's own common sense, should dictate his gradual rate of progress, and prevent a haphazard advance by leaps and bounds. Often pieces far too difficult for the student's skill are assigned to him by an unwise teacher—pieces which he is not yet prepared to master. This marks the beginning of so many of the bad habits acquired during practice. For in an effort to overcome difficulties beyond his power to vanquish the student now begins to play too fast. He is no longer capable of devoting proper attention to the correctness of his intonation, the quality of his tone, clearness in his passage-work, and thus he lays the foundation for a mode of playing void of order and balance, and a faulty technique.

True, there are those rare cases in which the pupil, by reason of great talent and unusual physical advantages, will, if his musical intelligence is on a par with his other qualities, rise far above the general level of student accomplishment. One is tempted then to put him to a decisive test. By way of experiment it is a good idea to set him a task well beyond his power, which will serve as a norm of measurement for determining his talent, and will show pretty clearly what he can do. If the experiment succeeds—that is to say, if after a certain length of time he has been able in satisfactory fashion to overcome the difficulties involved—he will have proven himself to be of the timbre of which virtuosi are made, and in thus developing his capacities he will have given an earnest of future success.

I myself tried an experiment of this sort for the first time in the case of Mischa Elman, then a boy of twelve or thirteen, and a pupil in my class in the Petrograd Conservatory. He had been chosen to play the first movement of the Tchaikovsky Concerto at a public examination. I was very well aware of the fact that the task would be a hard test for the child, yet I tried the experiment in order to see what he could make of it. At one of the rehearsals, some ten days before the examination, he could not manage to play a passage in thirds, in the cadenza. After having made him repeat the passage a number of times in succession, I told him he could not play the Tchaikovsky, and that he might as well prepare another piece. Whereupon, with eyes filled with tears, and in a voice full of determination, he assured me that at the examination the passage would go well, that he would be able then to play it in a manner that would satisfy me. I told him that I doubted it, in view of the short space of time left him for practice before the examination. But I did not want to discourage him; I wished to give him a chance. So I instructed him to get another piece ready for the rehearsal—one which he had mastered during the course of the year—but at the same time to perfect the Concerto. Then at the dress rehearsal he could play both numbers for me, and the question as to which of them he should play at the examination could be definitely settled. At the dress rehearsal he began with the Tchaikovsky—and there was no need of his playing the other piece, for the passage in thirds went perfectly.

In this case, thanks to the boy's extraordinary talent and energy, the experiment was a success. After that I knew all that might be expected of him, and the future proved that I was right.

Seven or eight years later, a case of the same sort presented itself—this time it was Toscha Seidel. He was then about as old as Elman had been at the time of the examination performances in Petrograd. Seidel was to prepare the Concerto No. 9 (D minor) by Spohr, in which the principal theme in the third movement is based on a succession of thirds, a passage which at that time was too much for the young student. The boy himself, as well as my assistant who aided him in preparing his lessons, opened their eyes wide when I assigned the work to him. They were not sure that they had understood me rightly. Yet, when two weeks had passed, Toscha Seidel came back to my class at the Conservatory, and played the third movement of the Spohr Concerto for me with absolute accuracy so far as intonation was concerned, and even with a certain abandon.

With Seidel as with Elman, the experiment which I had made had been entirely successful, and thereafter I knew just how to guide the boy until he made his *début*. But these cases are, of course, very much out of the ordinary, and cannot be regarded as examples to be generally followed. And even in the event of success in an experiment of this kind, one must content oneself with following the straight road, and advancing by degrees instead of by leaps and bounds.

My principle in general has been and still is to demand a great deal from my pupils, so that I can observe them, and come to a conclusion about them according to the manner in which they respond—or fail to respond—to my demands; and I have very often observed that spurring on the ambition of a student, making a certain achievement a point of honour, has produced excellent results.

CHAPTER VII

DOUBLE-STOPS—THE TRILL

I

SCALES IN THIRDS

To strengthen the fingers, and at the same time render them more supple, the student should pass on now to the scales in double-stops, but without neglecting the scales in single notes which we have already considered.

As soon as a certain degree of skill in playing these last has been acquired, as well as facility in changing from one position to another, the student may begin with thirds, taking them up first in the keys of C, G, D, A, and E major, very slowly. These

should be practised as indicated in the above example, both ascending and descending. By practising his scale in thirds in this way the student will be able to pay close attention to his intonation. Once accustomed to the double-stop, he may extend the exercise and play it as follows:

Then he may take the same scale on the strings D and A, playing it in G major; and also on the strings A and E, playing it in D major, always using the same fingering, and always paying close attention to the intonation and the change of positions.

Just as with the single-note scales, so in playing the scales in thirds the shift from one position to another should be effected in an inaudible manner—never accomplished by that slow gliding of the fingers which makes the connection disagreeably evident to the experienced ear. There is but one way to avoid this, and that is by keeping the second and fourth fingers in place and pressing the first and third fingers as close as possible against the other two and moving rapidly over into the third position.

When descending, the first and third fingers should remain in place, while the second and fourth approach as near as possible to them so that, when moving back swiftly into the first position, they fall quickly into place at the moment the first and third fingers are raised.

II

SCALES IN FOURTHS

I have often wondered why the compilers of treatises and "methods" on the art of violin playing, and those who edit collections containing every variety of scale, have omitted any mention of the scale in fourths?

Yet this scale in perfect fourths has importance for violinists from a technical point of view at least, and we meet it occasionally in chamber-music, orchestra-music and also in violin solos. Though a scale in perfect fourths is usually not encountered in its extended form (it is only on the seventh degree that the fourth changes from a perfect to an augmented one) it nevertheless has a real existence and a proper claim to every violinist's attention. Why then has it been ignored? Is it because a succession of fourths does not fall suavely upon the ear? Is it because the laws of harmony forbid? The answer to this question has hitherto eluded me, nor have I ever seen it raised in any collection of scale exercises. Nevertheless, the scale in fourths is exceedingly useful as an exercise for intonation.

The preceding exercise should be practised as written and in descending fourths as well, in various keys and also in the minor tonalities. The student will unquestionably find it considerably more difficult to play a scale in fourths in perfect intonation than he would to play scales in thirds, sixths, etc. On the other hand, if he applies himself to the task he will find it very much easier, later on, to learn to play flageolets (artificial harmonics), most of which are based on this same interval of the fourth, with a pure and perfect intonation.

I have observed that a great many students—even those who are well advanced from the technical point of view—find it difficult to play harmonics, without at all suspecting the real reason for their trouble. They retune their violins with the greatest care, put rosin on their bows, and yet their harmonics persistently fail to ring true. Then, at a loss to understand the source of their difficulties, they lose patience and pass on—and on the next occasion, they achieve the same unsatisfactory results.

In such cases I always advise the student to practise the scales in fourths, methodically, insisting that he pay attention to the position of the fourth finger. In addition it is absolutely necessary that the bow lie well on the strings without, however, forcing the tone. This course of procedure always solves this vexing practical problem—and I leave to future compilers of collections of violin-scales the task of answering the questions I have raised with regard to their negligence in the use of the scale in fourths.

III

SCALES IN SIXTHS

In both progressions of the scale in sixths, ascending and descending, I have my pupils keep one finger in its place—so far as it is possible. For when this finger is otherwise employed, so that both are raised at the same time, there is a vacuum, the vibration of one of the open strings is heard, and it becomes impossible to play a passage in sixths *legato*. But which finger is to be kept in place, in order to establish the essential connection on the gamut of the scale, is a point which each player can best decide for himself. If the student relies for guidance upon the various scale-fingerings given in books of scales, let him choose from among them the one best adapted to his individual needs. The young violinist will find in *Scale Studies in Double Stops*, by Alexander Bloch, and in H. Schradieck's *School of Technique, Book II*, valuable collections of material.

IV

SIMPLE OCTAVES (1–4 FINGERS)

The majority of students of the violin find that the playing of octaves (1–4 fingers) with the proper purity of intonation presents great difficulty. Yet this interval is one which recurs in every kind of music, and hence forms an integral part of violin technique. Sometimes it is the first finger which goes astray; in fact, it is usually the first finger which fails to perform its duty. Occasionally it is the fourth finger which makes a haphazard progress, or both fingers may hesitate, until the student, uncertain whether to advance or retreat, wavers, finishes his passage with a seventh or ninth, and is thankful if he does not find himself between these two intervals.

In order to conquer the difficulties in the way of the satisfactory playing of octaves I recommend that the student concentrate his attention exclusively upon the first finger, and give himself no special concern about the fourth. As a rule he tends to take exactly the opposite course, and in consequence the intonation is always dubious. I have my pupils practise octaves in such a way that though both fingers (first and fourth) are in place, the bow touches only the lower string (first finger), yet the fourth finger moving silently, in every sense of the word, exactly duplicates the action of the first.

In this manner the pupil's whole attention is concentrated on his first finger, and this is as it should be; for the first finger should serve to guide the fourth, and thus led, the latter finds the way without overmuch trouble.

It goes without saying that the movement of the two fingers should be carried out rapidly (even in a slow tempo), in order to avoid the horrible caterwaul of the *glissando* from one note to the other. In general, when it is a question of changing positions, the shift should sound, in the case either of single or double stops, exactly as though it had been made on the piano keyboard, as such a series would be played by a perfected artist.

V

FINGERED OCTAVES

Fingered octaves are, so far as I am able to discover, a product of the last quarter of the past century. There is a bare possibility, of course, that they were taught or used before that time, but so far as I am concerned I never, or at least only very vaguely ever heard them mentioned during my youth, and none of my teachers —neither **Hellmesberger**, Jacques Dont, nor Joachim (then in Hanover—during the reign of the blind King George, 1863–1865) —ever made me practise "fingered octaves".

It was not until later—when Wilhelmj played Paganini's D major Concerto, in which he introduced a scale of double "fingered" octaves in a cadenza of his own composing—that I heard them for the first time. Because of their novelty, and on account of the perfection and boldness with which Wilhelmj executed them those double "fingered" octaves produced a great effect. But to play them as he played them one would need his giant hand and his long, slender fingers.

But in the violin literature of the period there is no trace of double "fingered" octaves. Neither Paganini, Vieuxtemps nor

Ernst (excepting his transcription of Schubert's *Erl-King*), Wieniawski, nor Bazzini employed them in their works, which represent the flower of the virtuoso compositions of the time.

VI

TENTHS

In order to practise tenths successfully one need only follow the rules laid down for the first and fourth fingers in playing octaves. Short fingers will find the first position somewhat difficult because of the great stretch between the two fingers; yet if the left arm be well advanced towards the E-string, this difficulty may, nevertheless, be surmounted.

VII

THE TRILL

I have no hesitation in saying that a perfect trill is one of the virtuoso's most striking accomplishments. We have long trills and short trills, but whether they be long or short, this is essential —proper conformation of the hand and muscular strength doubled by an agility which endows the fingers with a degree of rapidity and endurance in movement approaching in effect that possessed by an electric bell.

There are some fingers which, blessed by a happy natural gift, experience not the slightest difficulty in carrying out a prolonged trill with perfect equality of movement. But there are other less fortunate fingers, which, in spite of long and assiduous practice,

50

never gain more than a mediocre mastery of the trill. Thus Wilhelmj, a great violinist, and one who shone by reason of his physical strength, had neither a good trill nor a good *staccato*. But to make up for it, he could draw from his Stradivarius the biggest and most powerful of tones, as I well remember, for I heard him in Russia between forty and forty-five years ago.

But Wieniawski and Sarasate, on the other hand, had a very precipitate and very even trill of great length which formed a brilliant factor in their technical equipment. Joachim shone principally in short, precipitate trills. Hence he played the Allegro of the Tartini sonata—known as "The Devil's Trill"— based on a short trill of this type, with inimitable mastery.

In order to secure a fine trill—either prolonged or short—the fingers must first of all be strengthened by gymnastic exercises, systematically carried out day by day. Practice material to develop this accomplishment is readily available in the collections of double-stop exercises already recommended, and to these may be added special exercises to strengthen the individual fingers. Naturally, to derive full benefit from this work, special attention must be devoted to those fingers which the student himself knows are weak—and this weakness of particular fingers is individual in every case. Whether it be your third and fourth fingers that are weak, or the first and second—or all of them— each of the weak fingers in question must be strengthened and trained separately, one after the other, while placing the three unoccupied fingers on different strings. (See Alexander Bloch's *Finger-Strengthening Exercises* and Schradieck's *Books I and II of School of Technique.*)

Raise the finger with a slow and even movement, then let it fall and strike the string—this without letting the hand take any part in the proceeding. Always remember in exercises for strengthening weak fingers that the fingers *only* should strike the string, and not the hand. Do not expect to overcome your difficulties all at once, and do not let want of success at the beginning discourage you. It is a matter of months, sometimes of years, of effort before certain muscular weaknesses can be overcome, yet, thanks to systematic hard work, you can eventually obtain if not a brilliant trill, at any rate a lovely and sonorous one.

For short and rapid trills in passages, the following exercise:

or else:

may be used.

For passages demanding a still more rapid movement, in place of a trill on two bowings (above), you may use a trill on a single bowing as follows:

I always make a point of teaching my pupils, however, that the melodic design should not be sacrificed for the sake of the trill which, after all, is only an ornament. In order to avoid this offence against musical taste, it is necessary always to complete the trill by returning to the note on which the trill began (consult the preceding examples), and to this end the violinist must observe the accent, which indicates the note to which one should return. This also holds good, at all times, with regard to the longer variety of trill.

VIII

THREE- AND FOUR-NOTE CHORDS

In playing chords the attack is the danger-point. The majority of young violinists believe that if they press the bow heavily against the strings, and bear down upon them with the arm, they will obtain a chord that is full and resonant. Exactly the opposite is the result, however. The bow-hairs, as a consequence of this pressure, suffocate and kill the vibration, and instead of a tone strong but pure, a species of scraping tone is given out, which, though greater in volume, is identical in quality with that produced when one attacks with a down-bow and unexpectedly makes the stroke with the entire breadth of the bow-hairs instead of only three-quarters of the bow-hair surface. Only an elastic wrist, and above all a tendency to remain midway between bridge and fingerboard, approaching the bridge rather than drawing away from it, will prevent the hand, when playing a chord, from falling back on the fingerboard and thereby producing a whistling, disagreeable tone. To sum up: (1) attack the chords from the wrist, using no more than three-quarters of the bow-hair surface; (2) press down lightly and try to keep the bow midway between bridge and fingerboard; (3) always attack two notes at a time, as follows:

CHAPTER VIII

ORNAMENTS—*PIZZICATO*

T H E Italian *mordente* and *gruppetto*—known in English as the "turn" and "grace-notes"—were the widely prevalent and freely used ornaments of the violin compositions of centuries past. They were mainly employed in airs, in slow movements whose expressive playing depended on the good taste and musical feeling of the artist. It is true that the use of ornamentation was overdone, yet this whole question of embellishment is an obscure one, and we have still to develop an authoritative body of rules which may serve as a guide to teacher and pupil. Now as in days gone by, the use of ornament in violin playing is taught in accordance with the individual teacher's point of view, and embellishments are played as the individual player's artistic good sense may dictate.

Even in his day, however, Leopold Mozart, the father of Wolfgang Amadeus, complained in his *Gründliche Violinschule*, that the solo violinists abused ornamentation to an extent which threatens the total extinction of the principal thing, the melody itself. Nevertheless, in the Concertos of Viotti and Paganini, we observe a gap, so far as ornamentation is concerned—one later filled in with elaborations and ornaments added by David, Wilhelmj, Kreisler, etc. Rode, Kreutzer and Spohr, however, carefully indicated the ornamentation in their works as they wished to have it performed and, strange to say, Johann Sebastian Bach and Mozart, all with meticulous care, embellished those portions and sections of their works which seemed to demand ornaments—to say nothing of Beethoven, the beauty and richness of whose ornamental *nuance* is incomparable. As a matter of fact, it is unnecessary for the player to change or add anything by way of ornament to the works of these great masters.

There are several varieties of ornament in violin-music. The *appoggiatura* or "grace-note", as may be seen in the following example:

In spite of the small notes the rhythm is not and should not be disturbed. These grace-notes, as notes, do not count in the rhythm, and in playing them the violinist should be guided entirely by his rhythmic sensibility. All ornaments of the kind, in fact, are subject to this law. The note with the cross-bar (*), is played quite short, while the unbarred note (**), borrows half the value of the note following it, but in such fashion that the rhythm remains unchanged save, of course, for the change in time-value of the note from which it borrows.

Then we have the *mordente* or "turn" of three notes:

in which the accent invariably falls on the long note. These mordents or "turns", however, are often marked with the sign ₩; as for instance, in the following example:

The principal rule to be observed by the player in slow movements and in *cantabile* sections is to avoid playing the turn too precipitately, and, above all, to make its rendition conform to the character of the musical phrase.

PIZZICATO

The *pizzicato*, or "pinching" of the strings, that is to say plucking them with the fingers, is a valuable violin effect, and is produced in two ways, by the right and by the left hand.

The right hand *pizzicato* is produced by the first finger of the right hand, the thumb supporting itself on the corner of the fingerboard, and the first finger plucking or "pinching" the string with the flesh of the fingertip and not with the nail. The string should not be jarred while pinching it, since this develops a disagreeable quality of sound. Let the string sound out fully and freely by attacking it in the direction of the G to the E-string, without effort, yet with the whole breadth of the fingertip, and only with its fleshy cushion. If this be done the resulting tone will have the quality of tone given forth by a harp-string when plucked by the finger of an experienced artist.

When properly produced the *pizzicato* is decidedly effective in orchestra music, chamber-music and solo compositions: for instance, in Beethoven's Grand Trio in B flat major, in the first movement; and the first movement of his String Quartet in E flat major, Op. 76. I mention these two works as examples in order to show how necessary a fine, sonorous *pizzicato* may be in the proper development of musical effect in an integral portion of a fine and serious work.

Distinct from the right-hand *pizzicato* is the precipitate *pizzicato*, which is produced by the fingers of the left hand. Rapid *pizzicato* passages are met with in Paganini's works as well as in the compositions of authors more recent, such as Ernst and Bazzini. When pinching the strings with the left hand, draw back the arm to the left, into a position which is the exact reverse of the usual position of the arm. Beyond all question, in order to be able to produce the *pizzicato* under consideration in a satisfactory way—and this holds good of every branch of violin technique—nature should have properly equipped one for the task. Thus, in this connection, the quality of the skin covering the fingertips plays an important part in the production of the *pizzicato* in question. If the player's skin be delicate and soft, the *pizzicato* will not sound out, while if the cushions of the fingertips are covered with a skin which is tougher and more resistant in texture, the *pizzicati* will ring out clearly and sonorously.

Let no student imagine that by forcing the pinching he will be able to draw a greater volume of sound from the string. He will merely be wasting his time in the effort. The only result will be a disagreeable, strident, grinding tone, and in addition, the skin of the finger will become irritated to such a degree that blisters may develop and prevent playing for several days.

CHAPTER IX

HARMONICS

NATURAL HARMONICS

N ATURAL harmonics—obtained from the open strings—
are present to the number of *four* on each separate string
of the violin. On the G-string, for instance, we have:

and similarly, these harmonics occur on the D-, A- and E-string.
The fingers indicated in the example or others may be used in the
different positions wherever they prove capable of producing the
same natural harmonic note.

ARTIFICIAL HARMONICS

The artificial harmonics are more difficult to play than the
natural ones, and practice in detail is necessary to play them and
produce the true harmonic effect. In order to master them, there
is one indispensable rule: they must be practised slowly, and
great care must be taken that the fourth finger, which produces
the harmonic (the first finger remaining firmly in place) scarcely
brushes the string in the perfect fourth, and that it be in exactly
the proper place. The slightest deviation as regards intonation
will result in a failure to sound the harmonic. When this occurs
the usual procedure is to blame the weather if it is raining, the
humidity if the sun is shining, or—if nothing else presents itself
as a suitable excuse—the temperature of the room in which one
chances to be playing. Or the hair, the rosin or the strings are

accused of being at fault! Whereas most frequently the failure results from the fourth finger—or both the fourth and first fingers —not being in the right place.

The consequences of this error are even more disastrous when a succession of harmonics in a slower or more rapid movement is involved. To avoid these difficulties, the student will do well first of all to practise the perfect fourth backward, so that his fingers will accustom themselves to a perfect intonation. For instance, as in the following exercise:

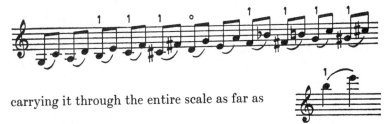

carrying it through the entire scale as far as

and back again, ascending and descending the scales in various keys. And to make doubly sure it is best to drill the fourth finger until it falls into place mechanically on the perfect fourth in any and every key, since artificial harmonics are played in all tonalities.

As to the bow, the attack must be made in a delicate manner, without forcing, and without throwing the stick on the string. A most important point to remember in this connection is that the fingers should be in position before the bow-stroke is made. See that the hand is at liberty to advance by degrees without any hindrance on the part of the bow, and then attack with the bow when the hand is in the desired position.

I will admit that this is complicated training, but the student who wishes to become a real virtuoso must resign himself to undertaking—and mastering—it in order to attain his goal.

DOUBLE HARMONICS

Long fingers and a large hand are the first essentials to the playing of double harmonics, on account of the wide distances between the various intervals, and the different strings which must be spanned. Besides this, perfect hearing, augmented by an instinct for absolute pitch, and a certain skill in the combination of intervals in each individual case are necessary.

There are three different groups of artificial harmonics: (1) those formed on the major third; (2) those formed on the perfect fourth (already mentioned); (3) those formed on the perfect fifth. These three intervals, combined with natural harmonics, supply the double harmonics. The following examples show simple artificial harmonics:

There is but little special material available for the methodical study of double harmonics,[1] the principal reason being, of course, because they are so rarely used. Besides, they require a hand and fingers naturally adapted to produce them, and they also presuppose seasoned nerves, able to endure the torture of notes frequently missed during practice. Yet even with all the natural aptitude and favourable physical prerequisites imaginable, there always remains a certain amount of risk in playing double harmonics in public. At times, when atmospheric conditions raise or lower the diapason, the strings will not stay in tune. In that event it is humanly impossible to make double harmonics sound, and no matter how skilful the performer may be, one or another will misfire, to the great astonishment of those of the audience who have no knowledge of the real cause of the catastrophe.

[1] There is a special treatise on harmonics included in Richard Hofmann's *Ecole de Violon* (the third or fourth part) and published by Zimmermann in Leipzig, which I knew in Europe.

CHAPTER X

NUANCE—THE SOUL OF INTERPRETATION
—PHRASING

THE average young violin student does not take to heart as he should the great importance of shading, of *nuance*, in music. He is inclined to believe that if he plays correctly, rhythmically, and perhaps with temperament, he is doing all a player can be asked to do. Nevertheless, he can never hope to be a genuinely accomplished violinist if he neglects that important phase of music which involves musical sensibility, a proper understanding of the composition to be played, and that great wealth of nuance of which the violin is peculiarly capable. A genius of Beethoven's calibre excels in teaching us how to shade, how to develop nuance. Study his quartets, his trios, his violin sonatas—not to forget his symphonies!—and you will find them replete with the greatest imaginable abundance of nuances. In addition to his great genius and power he insisted on bringing to his music all this varied and colourful wealth of shading. He did more: he was at particular pains to indicate these shadings by means of countless signs, in order to lend his compositions even more colour and greater animation than they would otherwise possess. For Beethoven knew very well that tonal monotony may easily impair the effect of any work—and I know of no other composer who has made such subtle use of nuance in general as he.

But the young student preoccupied with the technical possibilities of his instrument, is all too likely to forget this side of his art, which he should really regard from the first as an essential part of his technical development, and the sole means of raising his execution to an artistic level. The average student pays no attention to the difference between a *piano* and a *pianissimo*, to making sharp distinctions between *fortes*, *fortissimos* and *mezzo-fortes*, and above all he ignores the value of the *crescendo* and *diminuendo*, preceded by a *poco a poco*. As a rule he proceeds under the impression that *crescendo* means "louder", and that *diminuendo* stands for "softer", whereas these shadings should be carried out by degrees leading up to the *fortissimo* or down to the *pianissimo*, as the case may be, and sometimes developed, in one direction or the other, for a number of measures. Or, a *crescendo* may lead to a sudden *piano*. The *forte-piano* (fp)—which denotes that a strong attack is to be made followed by a sudden piano—is often indicated. The accent > is sometimes found stressing the strong, and sometimes the weak beat of the measure. I regard the proper presentation of this nuance as the very essence of all dynamic musical execution. The accent on the *forte* as on the *piano* is, after all, the indispensable means for all truly musical playing. I consider it so essential, in fact, that I believe that the accent should always be evolved out of the character and nature of the music itself, and should be specifically indicated by the violinist himself over certain notes in every composition in which the composer has omitted to make his own indications. An artist playing a work must resemble the orchestra conductor, who knows how to nurse along both his climaxes of expression as well as his dynamic climaxes.

If you wish to make a really favourable impression as a performer on the violin, you must avoid monotony and lack of colour, and only the introduction of the nuances and accents in their proper places will facilitate your efforts in this direction.

Monotony is the death of music. Nuance is the antidote for monotony. Berlioz once said: "The violin is capable of a host of apparently inconsistent shades of expression. It possesses, as a composite force, lightness and grace, accents both gloomy and gay, thought and passion. The only thing is to know how to make the violin speak."

"To make the violin speak"—those words sum up in a single phrase the whole matter of variety in expression. It is, of course, a generalization, but if its meanings be developed its truth will be apparent. In the orchestra, the great advantage the violin has over all the other orchestral instruments in expressiveness is due to the player's control of tone production and tone inflexion. He can make the violin speak, he can make it sing. He can run the whole gamut of emotions on its strings—if he can translate feeling into the expressional terms of dynamics and nuance, into tone graduation and the tone inflexion by means of rhythm, of stress, of musical shading.

I have compared the artist to the orchestral conductor, who is able to prepare and develop his emotional and his dynamic climaxes. And with the whole colourful and infinitely varied tone palette of the modern orchestral combination responsive to his slightest indication, the conductor, who plays upon this human key-board without having to pre-occupy himself with the actual physical production of its music, seems to have the advantage over the violinist. Yet the violinist, with only his four strings to draw upon, has within his far more limited range of tone volume almost equal opportunities for variety in expression. What he may lose in contrast in instrumental *timbres*—for he has only the violin tone to exploit, and cannot evoke the tonal quality of the wood-winds or brasses from the violin strings—he makes up again in the wonderful flexibility and variety of the violin tone itself. No wind instrument—the flute, the oboe, the clarinet—no matter how well played, can fail to produce an impression of monotony in solo performance, if heard long enough. This lies in the less flexible quality of its *timbre*. But the violin tone is capable of almost limitless variety in expression, if the tones are produced by a good player. It has even an advantage over other instruments of the string family itself in this respect. Take the 'cello, for instance. The 'cello is essentially a melody instrument, a lyric instrument. It is the baritone voice among the strings, and the sustained melodic line and not the brilliant coloratura passage is its natural mode of expression. It is true that there are exceptions to these rules: that a David Popper could exploit its higher registers in compositions strikingly effective in their swift tempos and brilliant passage-work; that a Pablo Casals can do anything, emotionally or technically, with the instrument, and make us forget while he is playing it that his instrument is a 'cello with the specific limitations of a 'cello, and remember only his mastery of the strings and string tone. But, generally speaking, the 'cello as a solo instrument lacks the *varied* possibilities of tone inflexion which the violin possesses. Beethoven wrote ten sonatas and a concerto for the violin—he wrote only five sonatas for 'cello.

And let the violin student never forget for a moment the splendid range of possibilities of varied expression of which his instrument is capable. For the greatest amount of application, the most unfailing devotion, the most imposing and comprehensive mechanical control of the violin are all of them well-nigh valueless without soul, emotion: and you can only communicate the soul of your music to your auditors through the medium of *nuance*, of shading. Certainly the violinist who plays a Mozart, Beethoven or Brahms *Adagio* and leaves his audience cold, is in no sense of the word an artist.

There are perhaps three means on which the violinist relies most for his nuance. Let us consider first the rôle that dynamics plays in interpretation. Dynamics, "the science of strength", as applied to music, is the system and theory which explains the various degrees of intensity or loudness of musical tones. A knowledge of it is a necessary part of the violinist's technical equipment, because of its importance as a factor in artistic playing. Ignorance of the exact meaning of the qualifying dynamic terms is inexcusable. I do not think, however, that the average student's ignorance of the meaning of the terms is responsible for his non-observance of them. I have already indicated my belief that the average student's delinquencies of this particular sort arise not because he does not know better, but because, in so many cases, he is not trained to a better observance, and has no clear realization of the very great importance of dynamic shading. He is too much absorbed in the actual playing of the notes. He does not pause to realize that *how* they are played really determines whether or not they are worth playing at all!

Timbre, quality and colour of tone, is another factor in *nuance* which the student must cultivate. There are no more beautiful violin effects than those arising from a properly varied and contrasted tonal colour. The violin tone is all string tone, yet each of its four strings has its own *timbre*, its own peculiar shade of colour, and probably no nobler example of the exploitation of the individual *timbre* of a single string can be found anywhere than in Bach's Aria for the G-string as arranged by Wilhelmj. Artistic gradation of tone-colour, of tone-quality, delights the ear just as artistic gradation of visual colour delights the eye. The *timbres* of any great living violinist are analogous to those of a Corot or a Meissonier. And quite as truly, in either case, whether violinist or painter, the absence of colour and of colour-variety in tone or on the canvas betrays the lack of genuine artistry.

Tempo is perhaps the third factor in the trilogy of factors to be considered under the general conception of *nuance*. And just as the dynamic signs are too little regarded by the student, so is he inclined to neglect *tempo* indications. He distinguishes roughly between a *largo* and a *presto*, an *adagio* or an *allegro*, but he is all too likely to overlook the hundred and one nuances of slower or more rapid movement which lie between such extremes, which he must himself feel to express. If he has no real notion of the infinite variety and meaning of tempo indications, with their infinite possibilities of shading, I would suggest that he pick up any good musical dictionary and get from it a conviction of the many gradations to which *tempo* is susceptible. Before he does anything else, however, let him acquaint himself with the three great classes of *tempi*. One class denotes a steady and equal rate of speed, from *molto lento*—than which there is no slower *tempo*—to *prestissimo*—which represents the apogee of rapid movement. In the second class we have all those *tempi* which indicate acceleration of movement, from *accelerando* to *veloce*; and in the third, from *rallentando* to *smorzando* are grouped the *tempi* of slackening speed.

And with *tempo*, with dynamics, and with colour as assembled to *nuance*, we must regard rhythm. If *tempo* denotes the rate of speed, the degree of movement, then rhythm may well be called the underlying soul itself of movement. Accent, on which I have already laid such stress, is really a rhythmic sensation. And rhythm and accent must be free, they must, in a certain measure, be instinctive and individual. A violinist without a sense of rhythm is no violinist, he is as helpless as a painter who is colour-blind. Rhythm is a principle underlying all life, and all the arts, not that of music alone. In violin playing it must be translated into natural interpretation in accordance with the character of the music. This rhythmic accent is as much of a necessity, in order to give the proper value to the details of musical phrasing, as it is in speech itself.

Nuance, then, expresses itself, or may be expressed, in terms of dynamics, *timbre*, and perhaps *tempo*, including rhythm. These are the mediums through which the soul of the player and the soul of the music which he plays are revealed to the auditor. Yet it is the law of the physical universe which determines this psychic expression. Nature herself underlies music as she underlies all other arts. And *nuance*—the principle of infinite change, variety, inflexion, shading, everywhere manifest in the physical world—is the vital principle in music. Yet in music, as in the other arts, it is difficult to determine where Nature ends and Art begins. The violin strings vibrate beneath the stroke of the bow, in accordance with the same principles which cause the strings of an Aeolian harp to stir in the breath of the wind. The hollow belly of the fiddle generates resonance in conformity with the same natural laws which cause the hollow tree-trunk to sound beneath the blows of the woodpecker's bill, and the overtones in a bird-note are evolved by the same acoustic phenomena as the harmonics drawn from the violin strings.

I regard *nuance* in music as the specific application of Nature's variability of mood and tone to musical ends and aims. Nature is never monotonous—the violinist who realizes the fact, and gives his playing those qualities of nuance which diversify Nature's every mood and aspect will never play in a stilted, tiresome fashion. His interpretation will never be conceived on a dead level of uniformity. Take Nature for a model—that is my advice to every player!

All *nuance* is already expressed in Nature, and Nature is a great teacher of *nuance*. The musician is especially susceptible to the appeal of natural beauty, since his art is one which allows the most vivid and varied emotional and imaginative expression, and has most eloquent means for such expression at its disposal. Composers of violin music, however, have often, in their imitation of Nature, developed the purely pictorial and programmatic at the expense of the higher and nobler ideals of pure music. Often they try to produce a mental picture or vision by suggestions directly influencing the ear, the reproduction of bird-songs, for instance, the whistling of the wind, or the rippling of the brook. But this type of Nature imitation in composition—which compels an analogous imitation in interpretation—does not stand for the noblest exploitation of Nature's possibilities.

More truly beautiful, more inspired is that music which aims, not by accurate imitation but by analogies in outline and *timbre*, to express some mood or moment of Nature, definitely expressing this purpose in its title, perhaps, or letting the relationship go unacknowledged and depending for effect upon the composition's value as "absolute" music.

In the interpretation of Nature-music which is purely external —that is to say purely programme-music—the violinist has a comparatively easy task. His interpretative scheme is already laid down for him; it is stencilled in the composition. *Nuance* in such a case is, more than anything else, a matter of intelligent attention to a detail already provided. But when Nature-music of a more subtle sort is to be played, or music which is absolute in character, then the matter of *nuance* assumes greater importance and calls for intenser study. Nature, by virtue of the principles which govern her expression in life and in art, illumines, particularly in the expression of rhythm and movement, of colour, light and shade, all absolute music as well as music which is either narrowly (as in the case of pictorial programme-music) or more subtly (as in that of suggestive programme-music) descriptive of herself.

Art begins where technique ends. But in interpretation, Art and Nature are twins. The violinist who listens to Nature and develops his *nuance* of interpretation out of her teaching will never become a violinistic automat. For Nature, ever changing, ever showing us some new mood, some new phase of her inexhaustible self, is the fountain-head of variety in expression.

In the standard editions of the works of the classic and modern violin masters, of course, the *nuance* of interpretation is indicated as fully and as comprehensively as possible. I have already spoken of the detailed wealth of *nuance* with which Beethoven has enriched his luminous pages. Earlier editions of Mozart's violin sonatas do not show this same meticulous care; but the work of succeeding interpreters has gradually established the interpretative values. And in practically all modern works the composers have fully indicated the *tempi*, the dynamic stresses and effects, the character of the movements, and the inflexions of tone to be observed. Yet with all these guideposts to point out the road to perfect interpretation, there still remains the widest room for individual latitude in expression, in colour, in emotional fervour, in dramatic intensity. I have already said that temperament is not a substitute for *nuance*—no violinist can interpret a composition in all its varied beauty by temperament alone—yet temperament, which is the special mental quality that lends individuality to performance, is always a valuable factor.

Individuality in *nuance*, however, should never degenerate into bizarre affectation. There is always a borderline, easily recognizable, where the temperamental oversteps the aesthetic bounds of propriety, and turns into caricature. I have always encouraged my pupils to be as individual as they could be in the interpretation of their repertory works; but I have never allowed them to carry originality to the excess of disfiguring beauty. The genuinely musical student, in most cases, is instinctively aware of this boundary which may not be overstepped. In some cases these offences against good manners in interpretation are the result of a commendable desire on the part of the student to follow closely the interpretation of some great virtuoso, to play the work as he has played it on the concert-stage. But it is, alas, only too easy to caricature, with complete unconsciousness and a sincere belief that one is improving one's interpretation, some great artist's interpretation of a movement or a passage. The slightest additional emphasis, the least extension of a *ritardando*, the tiniest exaggeration of a rubato, will often produce the most grotesque results, and the student, in his earnest effort to achieve a perfect replica of the expressional feature he is imitating, does not realize that he is worshipping the perversion of an ideal.

If the violinist can play Bach, Beethoven, Mozart, with the proper beauty of *nuance* their music demands, he need not fear any similar problems which the more modern works of the repertory may offer. The technical complexity of modern compositions is in many cases greater, they may make greater demands on the skill, the finger dexterity, the endurance of the player; but as regards interpretation—no! Take Bach, for instance. Bach's sonatas are quite as difficult to play as anything Paganini ever wrote—as hard to play with the proper *nuance*. There are no brilliant sweeps of double-harmonics, no *pizzicati*, no scales in fingered octaves; but their contrapuntal style, their polyphonic character, makes them extremely difficult to play perfectly. There are no finer studies for *nuance* existing than these same Bach Sonatas. In them you find singularly expressive principal themes, but they play hide and seek with each other in the complicated harmonic web, shifting from outer to inner voices and back again. The themal voices must be coloured, must be inflected, must stand out, must sing; yet at the same time the secondary voices—in their own sequence—must not be neglected; they must have their own proper place in the whole interpretative scheme. To play these Sonatas as they should be played, to interpret them with that wealth of *nuance* which makes their beauty, is very, very difficult. And it is for this reason that I say: If you can play the Bach Sonatas with the right shading then Lalo and Tchaikovsky need not worry you.

Too many students who are technically quite far advanced do not properly interpret the technically less difficult pieces they play, because they regard them as beneath serious consideration. This is a fundamental error in musical taste and judgment. No matter how simple, any violin piece worth playing at all is worth playing with the fullest amount of expression that music and player can give. Many of the lighter compositions used on the modern violin recital programme to give relief to more serious numbers do not look so difficult on the printed page, nor do they seem very difficult to play. But so often in these cases, because of the very fact that the musical idea in itself is slight, the whole musical effect of the composition lies in its interpretation. Without *nuance*—a *nuance* which gives beautiful, shifting highlights of contrasted *tempi* and colours—many of them would scarcely attract attention. Yet light, graceful trifles of this kind are so vivified, so coloured by the interpretation of the artist who plays them, that we forget their comparative musical slightness in the charm with which delicacy of shading and expressive playing invest them.

Yet all precept is vain without practice. Do not confine yourself to reading what I write of *nuance* and its supreme importance to the art of violin playing, meanwhile forming good resolutions that you will apply what you have read. The violinist, like every other artist, learns best by doing. In the study of the violin good

69

intentions unfulfilled merely lead us to procrastination, slovenliness, and a tendency to be content with oneself and one's achievements. Study *nuance* on the violin! Listen to yourself play! Play a phrase or a succession of passages in various ways, with varying inflexions, with changing emphasis, now softly, now loudly, until you have found the *natural* interpretation, until those factors which, collectively, make up what we know as *nuance* have merged in a harmonious entirety of expression. Rely on your own musical instinct while you are guided by the expression-marks of others!

True inspiration in music, the urge towards musical creation—whether it be of composition or interpretation—is dynamic, it is the creative influence of genius acting through the natural faculties, emotional, mental, spiritual. It is the longing for beauty expressing itself in the forms and with voices of art. And true inspiration—the inspiration of a Bach or Beethoven—harks back to Nature the divine, to that Nature which, according to a great writer, "is the Art of God". And this inspiration merely lies dormant in the printed page until we make it live and glow and radiate in tone. Each truly artistic performance of a Mozart, Beethoven or Brahms violin sonata is a fresh miracle. It awakes to the throbbing, moving, appealing life of tone all the loveliness hidden in those successions of black notes which are meaningless to the uninitiated. And in each reincarnation of such a work, on each occasion that its inspiration charms the auditory sense and moves the heart, it is the part of the player—the sorcerer, whose bow is his magic wand—to give it a soul. And this soul is interpretation—interpretation which is *nuance* in its final and perfected annealing of component factors in the matrix of individuality.

PHRASING

All music is made up of tones in rhythmic, melodic and harmonic order which appeal to our musical sense. And phrasing as applied to violin music is the art of giving musical phrases—whether they be themes, developments or passages in all their varied forms—the right degree of relief, the right allotment of shading and emphasis, with due regard for their melodic and rhythmic character and for their interrelation. The musical phrase on the violin is naturally a melody-sentence. It may be two, four, six, eight measures long, or even longer; the point being that it forms an uninterrupted sentence in which its composer develops his thought and his feeling.

The violinist must always remember, however, that the individual musical phrase or sentence—just like a sentence in a book—is but a single unit of the entire melody-line. It is important only in proportion to its importance in the melody-line taken as a whole. The secondary value of modifying or subordinate phrases must be evident in the violinist's playing of them; he must never, tonally or in expression, elevate them to the level of importance equal to that of his principal phrase or phrases. An appreciation of these relative values is the first great principle of all phrasing. When studying a composition for the first time, it is absolutely essential that the student try to grasp the idea as a whole, that he get a clear mental conception of its general structure as well as of the relations of phrase to phrase before attempting to give a final interpretation of the character of the work.

The dead level of monotony which we notice in the performance of some violinists is, in the main, due to a lack of proper phrasing. They seem content to play the notes as they are written, and apparently do not realize that a melody is something more than a long string of tones to be sounded in succession. In all music there is an underlying skeleton of form. The melody is not a projection of successive notes; it is carefully and consistently built up of melodic units, each of them independent, yet all dependent on each other, and calling for varying degrees of rhythmic and emotional accentuation. Even in the short melodic phrases of the modernists, which are not subjected to the balance of classic formal rules in their inception, there is an inner musical law of proportion which makes their proper phrasing all the more imperative.

Phrasing, as regards execution—that is, from a technical standpoint—is principally a matter of correct bowing and fingering—always supported, however, by artistic feeling. Phrasing may properly be regarded as a very specific application of *nuance*— for phrasing is in the broadest sense tonal shading and inflexion

71

combined with rhythmic delineation—all of which applied to compositions as a whole resulting in what is known as "a correct interpretation". Phrasing is always something essentially personal. It has really no fixed laws—though various conflicting systems of phrasing exist—and depends wholly on the musical and the poetical sense of the performer. The convincing speaker, as a rule, does not depend on elaborate oratorical laws in order to move or impress his hearers. If he understands, if he feels what he is going to say, his explanatory and qualifying sentences fall naturally into place, the strong phrases in his address stand out in high relief.

In the same way phrasing for the violinist should not be a matter of rhythmic elocution. His musical taste, his musical intelligence, his musical sense of proportion must guide him in his phrasing. No two artists phrase the same passage in exactly the same manner; their phrasing may be similar, yet there will always be delicate distinctions, minute variations, qualifications, differences due to their individual temperament, the individual quality of their inspiration, and—not to be forgotten—their knowledge and skill as well as their instinct.

But how is the young violinist to determine whether or not he phrases well in his playing? He can only be guided by the effect actually produced on some person who reacts sensitively to music. Since that is the only means by which he can hope to come to a decision, I regularly say to my students: "Listen to your phrasing! Let your instinct, your musical good sense, your own reaction to your phrasing tell you whether your conception is right or wrong!" Correct phrasing is one of the hall-marks of true artistry, and only that violinist who has a fine and true conception of phrasing displays the quality of his talent in the most favourable light and takes rank among the artists.

All really beautiful phrasing depends, of course, in the last analysis, on technical perfection. For no matter how fine the student's musical instinct and his sense of proportion may be, faulty bowing—and faulty fingering as well—will inevitably destroy the continuity which is the very essence of smooth and convincing phrasing, and result in misrepresentation of the composer's ideas and intentions. Without technical competence even the most gifted interpretative instinct must fail of practical application.

72

NUANCE

Phrasing, like other more aesthetic branches of the art of violin playing, is one of those things for which a detailed scheme of instruction cannot well be laid down. It is almost impossible to make specific suggestions for phrasing. It can be demonstrated, violin in hand, but not described. Furthermore, the violinist is characteristically so dependent on the mood of the moment, the accidental influence of temper and disposition, that the same musician seldom plays the same phrase twice in exactly the same manner.

The principal point for every student to bear in mind is that good phrasing presupposes an artistic building-up of musical interest looking forward to a climax. If he will remember this, and rely on his natural musical instinct, his good taste and feeling for proportionate values, he cannot go wrong.

CHAPTER XI

STYLE

BUFFON once said: *Le style est l'homme même* (Style is the man). I believe that style in literature is the author, and certainly in music it is the musician himself. In fact, where is the musician deserving of the name who does not possess the instinct for style in music? What sort of violinist would he be who played all the masters, all the various kinds of music, in the same way? In dramatic art style is essentially the element of declamation. Music also calls for declamation—interpretation— based on a thorough understanding and grasp of the character of a composition. All the composer's indications serve this one purpose—they exist to make possible a rendering of the composition which shall be in keeping with its character. Whether that character be lyric or dramatic, heroic or passionate, gay and care-free, its proper delineation always requires a variety of accents, energetic stresses or tender, delicate touches.

To understand and to cause to be understood—this is the aim to which the performing artist must aspire. The music-loving public in general is very sensitive and is readily impressed by genuine art, if art be presented in such wise that its beauties can be grasped.

The innumerable music-festivals and concerts throughout the land attest this fact. What a mixed public these festivals attract, yet the majority of works performed at them are works of solid artistic value. And when the great artists—as they now so generally do—play a piece of music by Bach or Beethoven, presenting it absolutely in character, the crowd is impressed and reacts even more frankly and more gladly to its beauties than does the so-called musical connoisseur or professional musician, who has his own well-established ideas regarding the works of the great masters, and is usually convinced that his conception is the only true and right one. The performer, however, may be said to have reached the apogee of his art when he is able to give an ancient or modern composition its true character in his performance, lend it the colour with which its composer has endowed it. If, in addition, he is capable of merging in his own temperament the author's original thought, if he can react himself to the beauty of the work or phrase, he need have no doubt of his capacity to play the composition in a way that will impress others. For the violinist whose technique is assured, and who possesses that peculiar magnetism which exerts irresistible and convincing charm, is able to sway the greatest audience with compelling power—like the Hebrew prophets and the great masters of the plastic arts, like the great poets of ancient and of modern days, the public speakers of all ages—in a word, like all other artists whose appeal is addressed to the multitude.

Style in music, as in the other arts, is the mode or method of presenting the art in question in a distinctive and intrinsically appropriate way. The word style is used freely in discussing both literature and music, and it is often used carelessly. The old Romans used a *stilus*, an instrument of wood, metal or ivory, to engrave their thoughts on tablets of wax. And when they spoke of "turning the stilus", they meant to imply that they had modified what they had written with the sharp end of the stilus by erasing with the blunt end. In music the violinist "turns the stilus" when he applies blunt, judicious self-criticism and correction to his playing; when he realizes that it can be improved—and acts upon his conviction. In the old days everyone who used a *stilus* wrote in a different and individual manner, and his writing gave as clear an indication of his temperament and character as the playing of the violinist expresses his own individuality—from his every interpretation of a musical work, to the way in which he picks up his instrument, or lets his fingers fall upon the strings. Just as you could see the Roman scribe's character revealed by the lines drawn with his *stilus* in the wax, so the temperament, the distinctive features which make up the musical character of the violinist, are disclosed by *his* musical *stilus*, the bow, as he draws it across the strings. This is the essential meaning, then, of Buffon's phrase, "Style is the man", when it is applied to music.

I have referred to the individual magnetism which the violinist must possess if he is to sway his listeners. This quality of personal appeal based on individual power or charm has always seemed to me to be the real foundation of all style in violin playing. There is no one definitely established way of playing a given work by a master, for there is no absolute standard of beauty by which the presentation of a violinistic art-work can be judged. A type of playing extravagantly admired and cultivated in one age may be altogether rejected in another. The general aesthetic sense and sensibility of the period in which we ourselves live, our own contemporary feeling for what is true and acceptable in musical style is the only standard of judgment to which we can refer the artist's interpretation. If the violinist satisfies this aesthetic taste of ours (for there is no absolute standard of beauty) and if he moves us, if he convinces us, if he makes us feel that he is revealing to us beauty's true soul—then his interpretation is justified, his style is faultless. The great living violinists can wake the overtones of our heart-strings today: Tartini similarly moved the listeners of his time, and the style, the interpretation of each is and was true to the aesthetic demands of their contemporaries. It is impossible to make any adequate comparison of the playing of these artists. For one thing, no man still living is in a position to describe Tartini's playing from actual hearing. Yet, wonderful as his playing must have been, if we are to judge by the accounts of it which have come down to us—he was popularly supposed to have sold his soul to the devil in order to become the greatest violinist in the world—it is a question whether, were Tartini himself to appear in recital today, a twentieth-century audience would be enthusiastic over his playing. The gap between the aesthetic concepts, the musical concepts, the critical values of his time and our own is too great to be easily bridged. But Tartini—like his pupil Nardini, and like Viotti, who "drew a bow of cotton across the strings with the arm of a Hercules"—was justified in his individual style by the aesthetic judgment of the music-lovers of the time in which he lived, and in the absence of any absolute standard this verdict must be accepted for the past, just as we accept the aesthetic sense of our own time as competent to pass on the merits of the artists of the present day.

I have always found it impossible to regard style in music as a matter of historical development, however. Beauty and not tradition is the touchstone of all style. And what may be beauty in style during the eighteenth century is not necessarily that in the twentieth. I have no respect for that much-abused word "tradition" in the sense in which it is largely used. If respect for tradition were carried to its logical conclusion, we should still be living in the Stone Age, doing as our forefathers had done before us. Tradition in music, as in all else, is the antithesis of progress, it is the letter which kills the living spirit. The truth of one age is bound to be modified by the events of another, for truth is progressive. The aesthetic truth of one period—the interpretative truth of one generation—may be accounted a falsehood by the tenets of the next. For each age sets its own standards, forms its own judgments. There is no doubt but that Tartini stood for the truest expression of the beauty of violin playing, for the best example of style, in the broadest sense of the word, of his epoch. And if he could play for us today whatever there were in his art, in his interpretation, in his style that appealed to us as beautiful would still be beautiful after a lapse of some three hundred years. But that which we could not accept would be faulty—though it might have been beautiful for his own times.

Tradition in reality weighs down the living spirit of the present with the dead formalism of the past. For all these hard and fast ideas regarding the interpretation of older classic works, their tempi, their *nuances*, their expression, have become formalisms, because the men whose individuality gave them a living meaning have disappeared. The violinists of today are rightly just as individual, each in his own way, as were those of the past. Let them play as they honestly feel they must, let them give us beauty as they—and we—understand it. Let them express themselves, and not fetter their playing with rules that have lost their meaning. Let them not hamper that most precious individual quality the artist has—his style—with the dusty precepts handed down from times gone by. Beauty we must have, tradition we can dispense with. How is a violinist to conceive the meaning of an older work which he may be studying if his own musical instinct, his freedom of conception, are obfuscated by the dictum: "This must be played in such and such a manner, because so and so played it that way two hundred years ago?"

One tradition only do I recognize—that it is the function of the artist to enter into the spirit of a composition, and reveal to us the intentions of its composer.

The musical message of the composer, the true spirit of his inspiration, the soul of his music—that is what we are interested in. Though no two great artists now playing before the public interpret the Bach *Chaconne*, let us say, in exactly the same manner—yet hearing either the one or the other, at different times, we may nevertheless feel that the true inwardness of Bach's music has been presented to us in each case. And what more can we ask? Are we to deny the beauty of their interpretation, which we hear, by which we are moved, because someone who has never heard Spohr himself play the same work, but who has carefully collected statistical evidence to establish his "traditional" rendering, explains that Spohr's interpretation must be considered the only vital one, being "traditional"?

If the artist has entered fully into the spirit of the composition he is playing, and if we accept his reading of its spirit, if as it sounds from his strings, we feel its truth, its beauty, its poetry, then it has been read aright, and we ask no more. And the artist who accomplishes this has solved the question of musical style.

For style in music is not identical with style, for instance, in architecture—though architecture has been called "frozen music". In architecture style means the exact definition of and differentiation between varying types of structural art, of various countries and different periods. And we still erect buildings in the Ionic style, the Egyptian style, the Gothic style, the style of the French Renaissance, in this twentieth century. But style in music, in the interpretation of music, is not a series of sharply defined orders. There is, from my point of view, only one style— no matter how varied its individual interpretations may be—and that is what contemporary understanding and appreciation generally admits is the just and unique expression of musical beauty presented by its interpreter. No violinist can properly say: "I will play this work in the style of Corelli, in the style of Rode, in the style of Paganini." The individual modes or manners of these violinists, each in his own period contributing to make up the style of that period, have passed. We know them no more; such an effect could and would convey the idea of style as I understand it today, only in so far as through its use musical truth and beauty were made audibly apparent to us.

The plastic arts, unlike music, have the advantage of practical immortality. Notre-Dame Cathedral in Paris presents the same appearance today as it did when first completed in 1240. But it is a question whether any of the music sung at its solemn dedication is to be found even in the manuscript collections of museums or libraries, to say nothing of the interpretation of that music. The Sphinx has survived by many centuries Rameses's triumphal hymns. St. Sophia, at Constantinople, is still outwardly the same as when the Emperor Constantine erected it; but Byzantine music, a rich and elaborate system, is reduced to the paleographic fragments which musical antiquarians exhaust their ingenuity in deciphering and collecting. Music is a pictorial art whose pictures are evanescent, though ever renewed. An art of the centuries, it nevertheless lives only in the expression of the moment. Style in musical interpretation cannot therefore be crystallized into set formulas of a plastic art—it is liquid, ever in process of transmutation. The style of each period of musical history is summed up in the various individual projections of music which have been heard and accepted as valid by the period itself. And it is this factor of individuality in musical style which makes it dynamic rather than static.

The very nature of his instrument, the peculiar personal character of his physical and musical endowment, of his genius and temperament, compel the violinist to project beauty in an individual manner. Does Elman play the Tchaikovsky Concerto in the same style that Heifetz plays it? How could he? Each violinist is individual, and his each interpretation is individual— each may present the same music with the richest variety of technical and musical effect, and still play it in an altogether different manner.

Consider the wide variety of music written for the violin—and the different men who composed it. There are the concertos, for instance, of Bach, of Mozart, of Beethoven, of Mendelssohn. Are not all of these compositions individual, do they not all unmistakably reflect their composers? Bach—the great contrapuntal master, who always thought of music in terms of the organ; Mozart—gay, tender, always in love; Beethoven—having the cosmos in his breast; Mendelssohn—the perfect gentleman, in his music as well as in his life. No two of these masters resemble each other; each of them must be interpreted in accordance with his own manner. How then would it be possible to play them all in the same fashion? For they have but one thing in common—their greatness.

This same wide divergence, this absolute difference in the kind and quality of their imagination, in the type and manner of their performance, cannot help but exist in their interpreters. To a pedantic interpretation of a Beethoven violin concerto, one based on carefully collated "traditional" evidence, and prepared with that conscientious lack of imagination which is so often the enemy of all beauty, I should prefer an ardent temperamental reading, one quite unsupported by any traditions, yet in which the artist pours out his very soul in the honest endeavour to grasp that of the master. He might exaggerate, he might be guilty of over-emphasis—but his interpretation would be a living one, it would speak to the heart! I think that Beethoven himself would choose such an interpretation.

Historical style, traditional style: I acknowledge that there are such things, just as we have armour in museums and time-hallowed observances. And I will not withhold due respect to all musical tradition which serves a useful purpose, which is a contribution to the general history of music. Style, however, is incidental to its period. It changes but does not develop—I am speaking as a violinist, of violin playing—in the sense that its development is sequential. How can it? Style in reality is the temporary crystallization, at various periods, of the ideals of violin interpretation best suited to the intellectual and musical feeling of the periods in question, *and born of the violin music of those periods itself.* No doubt it has even in a measure been influenced by the make of the instrument. Speaking in a general way, the high model violins, such as those of the Stainer type, speak more readily, while the flatter violins of the Cremona school have more carrying power and flexibility, and their tone is more susceptible to subtle variations by the player. That the greater interpretative possibilities of the Cremona type have had their favourable influence on violin composition is more than probable. But this is only incidental. The music written for the violin by the older masters, and played by them, did far more to determine the style of their period.

Another century, other music—other music, another style. Of course we do not play Bach as we play Tchaikovsky. But that is not really because tradition tells us that Bach requires a different interpretation. Musical instinct is sufficient. We play Bach differently because his music itself makes us observe certain canons of taste, certain modes of expressional procedure in presenting his Sonatas or his Concertos. But I again insist that it is not because of any traditional feeling—at least it should not be—for Bach's works rise far above all considerations of historical style in their grandeur and majesty, their soul and charm. We play them, or try to play them, as Bach's music should be played—reverently, almost as a rite of the sacrosanct mass of beauty, expressing as best we may, individually, all that they convey. Probably no great violinist of today plays the Bach sonatas as they were played by the well-known violinists of Bach's own day. Yet, despite the fact that the player may be centuries removed from the interpretative spirit of Bach's time, he may play Bach sonatas better than they were wont to be played then. The *musical* spirit of Bach transcends all narrow limitations of period, and the artist of today who truly enters into this spirit will play Bach as he should be played, and will play Bach better because he will play him in the interpretative spirit of our own generation, not that of 1720.

And in that very period, the eighteenth century—which blind upholders of "tradition" regard with the awe which the poor in spirit reserve for what they regard as established fact—the Abbé d'Olivet first used the expression "to form one's style"—the direct negation of the idea that style is the outcome of tradition. It is true that he used the expression *à se faire un style* in a literary sense. But it is every whit as applicable to music. The violinist *must* form his own style, and his style *must* be, more or less, the expression of his own individuality. Tradition represents the attempt to impose on oneself the individuality of another. Voltaire, who was anything but a devotee of the theory of the sacredness of what is handed down, declared that "style lends distinction to what is most ordinary, strengthens what is most feeble, infuses what is most simple with grandeur". Musical style, in its true sense, does as much for music. And these keen minds, able then to define style in a manner so consonant with our ideas of today, lived during the very eighteenth century whose supposed traditions are so frequently invoked by the pedantic to justify interpretations whose vitality passed with their era. And these same traditions, as they are now termed, no doubt represented in their own day—the eighteenth century—innovations to which the upholders of the good old traditions of the sixteenth and seventeenth centuries probably objected strenuously. How can we doubt that when Tartini was making a practical application of those discoveries of his regarding the theory of bowing which marked an advance on previous usage, and delighted his audience with his double-stops, trills and other novel violinistic effects, some old conservatives were talking about the "traditions laid down" by older (and hence, of course, better) composers such as Massimiliano Neri and Tommaso Vitali. And if there were any violins and violinists before 1550— which is very doubtful—those who followed them in the course of another generation were probably informed, in turn, of the superior value of tradition over individual development.

My own belief is that too great a preoccupation with style as such tends to hamper its fullest and freest expression in the individual player. Do not think of style—think of expressing the soul of music in the most moving and appealing way, with the richest variety of *nuance*, with the greatest sincerity—and you have your style. The manner in which you express the music you are playing (technique I take for granted), is only a part of style; colour, warmth, emotion, temperament, intuition, the feeling for delicate changes of mood, abandon, a thousand and one factors all must unite to form a modern style, one adequate to do justice to the great varied repertory of standard works, old and new, which form the literature of the violin.

A student's acquisition of certain technical tricks and individual mannerisms—whether they be mannerisms of bowing, of expression, of interpretation copied from some famous virtuoso or teacher—does not for a moment imply that the student who has copied them really plays in the master's manner. Imitation may be the sincerest form of flattery—but any student who flatters a master in this way is doing so at the expense of his own individual development. His jackdaw mannerisms may in the course of time become second nature, but they will still be mannerisms—whereas in the case of the violinist in whom they are inborn they are not necessarily mannerisms, but a veritable part of his stylistic outfit.

I have already said that the violinist must enter into the spirit of a composition—but he must not try to enter into it in disguise, in borrowed clothes, tricked out with foreign technical and expressional odds and ends, products of his observation of his more illustrious compeers. The interpretation of a great work (or even of a small one, for that matter) should be approached in a spirit of reverence. We do the greatest honour to art when we offer our own very best, not the best we can borrow from someone else. And the communion between the spirit of the music and the soul of the interpreting player must be immediate; it must not be complicated by the player's attempt to express the music by means of someone else's bag of tricks.

Forget tradition. Dismiss the idea that you must try to play such and such a work just as so and so plays it. Do not think of style! Concentrate quite simply and honestly on putting your whole heart and soul into the task of making the music you are playing live, expressing it as *you* feel the composer meant it to be expressed. And do this with reverence, with devotion. After all, the artist's first study of some masterpiece of violin literature, his first performance of it, if he be a true artist, is somewhat in the nature of a sacrament. The worshipper is approaching a new dispensation of musical beauty—and such are holy. He should be like the Mohammedan who leaves his slippers outside the mosque when he enters into Allah's sanctuary—and he should remember, too, that it is his *own* slippers the Mohammedan leaves outside the mosque, and not someone else's.

I have taught for many years and I still take pride in the fact that I have always insisted on the one great principle—that my pupils express *themselves*, and that they must not try to express me. Elman, Zimbalist, Heifetz, Seidel, Kathleen Parlow, Eddy Brown, Max Rosen, Thelma Given, Ruth Ray, Michel Piastro—is not each and every one of them distinctly different from every other? Has not each and every one of them his own strongly marked individuality as a player, and his own individual style? I have never tried to mould my pupils to any narrow aesthetic theories of my own, but only to teach them the broad general principles of taste out of which individual style develops. As regards interpretation I have always encouraged them to find *themselves*. I have always allowed them all freedom except when they have tried to sin against the aesthetic principles of art.

At the beginning of this chapter I intimated that style in violin playing, in all music, is in its essence declamation—the expression of the character of the music played with every inflexion that dramatic verity or lyric feeling suggests. And this, again, is in essence no more than making beauty live, making inspiration luminous, making the auditor understand the loveliness lying dormant in the printed page by means of the player's own sympathetic understanding of it, and by means of his projection of that understanding with strings and bow.

So I once more repeat: to understand, and to cause to be understood—these words sum up the end and aim of style. The violinist whose playing is like a light in the darkness, who makes his auditors feel the beauties he himself feels, has learned the ultimate lesson of style. For style in this true sense is not the outcome of tradition; it proceeds from the wellspring of individuality. It is not dammed and dyked-up pedantic formalism, but flows undefiled, as free and unconstrained as beauty itself.

CHAPTER XII

THE NERVES AND VIOLIN PLAYING

HAVING touched on the numerous other qualifications—both psychological and physiological—which go to make up the apparatus perfectly adapted for learning to play the violin properly and well, I must not fail to speak of the important part played by the nerves and nervous condition of young students—and even of great violinists on the concert-stage—as affecting their activities in their chosen field. The importance of the violinist's nervous condition may be gathered from the fact that when it is unsatisfactory, it oft-times opposes an insurmountable barrier to his success as a virtuoso.

My own opinion is that there exists no remedy, either hypnotic or medical, which is capable of curing or even temporarily paralysing the effect of that form of nervousness known as "stage-fright" in those who are subject to it. There are cases of unconscious nervousness, which develop some hours preceding the artist's actual appearance on the stage. These are most frequent in quite youthful artists who are subject to it without being aware of the fact. The culmination of the attack is manifested in a variety of ways. In some instances when these players finally appear before their audiences they hurry their tempo immeasurably; in others, on the contrary, they will play the various movements of a concerto, a sonata or a composition of any kind as though they found it very hard to go on. There are some even who under the influence of this nervousness actually reverse their tempo, and play a movement noticeably faster or slower than they have already taken it—which is likely to disconcert an audience which has been looking forward to hearing a repetition of some favourite number. And if some young student has attended the concert in the hope of learning how the piece in question should be played, he is likely to go away without knowing which of the two renditions is the one he should follow.

VIOLIN PLAYING AS I TEACH IT

I remember that Hans von Bülow, before he went out upon the stage, always rubbed his hands together feverishly. If someone, during such moments, asked him a trivial question, von Bülow either repulsed him sharply or else turned his back upon him without a word, and continued rubbing his hands. Anton Rubinstein, before he made his appearance on the concert platform, always strode up and down the room like a lion in a cage, and, strange to say, he looked like one as well, owing to the expression of his face and the magnificent head of hair which hung about his head like a mane. He was quite as unapproachable as von Bülow at such times, but he lacked the latter's sarcastic and disagreeable manner. One evening, at Petrograd, he was to play one of his own Concertos—I think it was the No. 5 in E flat. I was to accompany him, being at the time conductor of the symphony concerts of the *Société Musicale Russe*, which Rubinstein himself had founded. At the dress rehearsal— which was a public affair and for which the hall was overcrowded —his nerves were so agitated that he made mistakes and began to stumble. After the rehearsal the crowd was so great that I found it impossible to talk to him. But the evening of the concert, not being quite certain whether he had made intentional changes in his playing or whether there had been a mistake on his part, I went to consult him, score in hand. Rubinstein, however, without interrupting his agitated promenade for a moment, seized me by the arm, closed the score and said: "I know no more about it than you do; but both of us are musicians, and we will keep together no matter what happens." And, in fact, he played marvellously well that evening.

Those who were fortunate enough to hear him play for an intimate circle of friends, though, were really the only ones who could form a competent opinion regarding the magnitude of his genius. It was on such occasions that he displayed the full grandeur of his conceptions, and gave himself up completely to his divine inspirations, forgetting himself and all else in order to play as none had ever played before.

Joachim was also extremely nervous on the stage. He himself told me that when he played for the first time at the *Concerts du Conservatoire* in Paris—then the most celebrated symphonic concerts in all Europe, at which the most famous artists

86

considered it an honour to play gratuitously—he was to render
the Beethoven Concerto, which was, so to speak, his war-horse,
and which he played continually. But on that occasion the great
Joachim was so nervous that—to use his own words—he lost the
use of his faculties to such an extent that he actually did not
know that he had completed the first movement of the Concerto,
and it was not until the plaudits of the crowd brought him back
to himself and he began the second movement, the *Larghetto*,
that he felt at ease. Once, when he paid one of his rare visits to
Petrograd, I had an opportunity of observing Joachim in the
throes of a nervous crisis. He was playing the Beethoven Concerto already mentioned, and I was conducting the orchestra
accompaniment. From the very start I felt that his bowing was
not calm; and when he reached the final trill, on a sustained
note, which closes his own *cadenza* of the first movement, his
bow trembled so that, though he had not as yet reached the
end, I did not wait for him to play the concluding turn of the
trill, but signalled the orchestra to fall in with the perfect triad.
To this day I recall with pleasure the look of satisfaction he
gave me.

I myself, from my earliest youth to the very last time I
appeared in public, have always been very nervous, and this
nervousness did not leave me until the first composition on a
recital programme or the first movement of a concerto with
orchestra accompaniment had been played.

The younger generation of virtuosi now before the public
would seem to be better fitted for the struggle. Mischa Elman,
who went to Berlin to make his *début* at the age of fourteen,
began his career with an unusual experience. The night before the
recital he was unlucky enough to sleep in a hotel bedroom heated
by a charcoal stove. Both he and his father were well-nigh
suffocated by the coal-gas fumes when the latter, waking up in
the middle of the night, his head confused, still had sufficient
strength to open a window and thus save his son's life and his
own. Only a few hours later, sick, hardly able to stand on his
feet, the young violinist made his *début*. It was the beginning of
his virtuoso career.

Jascha Heifetz, playing for the first time in San Diego, flew
there from Los Angeles by aeroplane, arriving three hours before

the concert, to the great astonishment of his manager, who was expecting him at the railway station.

Toscha Seidel has himself informed me that he feels entirely at ease the moment he steps out upon the stage.

It would almost seem that some changes must have taken place in the nervous systems of concert violinists, if we are to judge by the younger generation of virtuosi. Or are there violinists among those who are unconsciously nervous? For these instances which I have cited are by no means isolated ones. Eddy Brown, also, knows what stage fright is only by hearsay. And Zimbalist has told me that he is greatly agitated *before* coming on the stage. Is this merely because they are young, and will these fortunates be obliged to pay nature's debt of nerves later on?

CHAPTER XIII

THE VIOLIN REPERTORY OF YESTERDAY AND TODAY

DURING the past forty or fifty years a remarkable evolution has taken place in the repertory of the virtuoso violinists. This I attribute to the unusual quality of good music of every variety produced and played during that period. For in every civilized land great symphony orchestras, choral societies, chamber-music groups, and other organizations and institutions devoted to music have been offering the masses an opportunity of hearing the best music in popular concerts. Little by little, acquaintance with good music has developed wider general appreciation of it, has raised the level of popular taste, until now the music-loving public is no longer willing to content itself with the limited repertory of the old-time virtuoso. No programme which has only superficial value—which fails of any sound intrinsic merit save the dubious one of throwing into sharp relief the technical excellencies of the individual violinist—is going to be received with enthusiasm by the modern audience whose ear has been trained to good music.

The motto "Music exists because of the virtuoso" has been disavowed, and "The virtuoso exists because of music" has become the credo of the true artist of these later days. There was some justice, however, in that earlier contention, for, following the example of Paganini, his contemporaries, and the virtuosi who succeeded him, generally made a practice of composing their concert repertories themselves—this with the intention of flattering the more or less uncultivated taste of the masses. These compositions were conceived for the express purpose of displaying to advantage the individual virtuoso's technical achievements; the purely musical side was regarded as negligible so long as the composition guaranteed an ample reward of personal success.

89

Paganini, for instance, in spite of the novelty of idea, the elegance and harmonic richness and variety of his compositions, conceived them almost purely from the point of view of violinistic effect. His music was skilfully devised to display to the greatest advantage his stupendous skill in playing harmonics and double harmonics, extended passages in double-stops, his mastery of the G-string, his intimate combination of bow-sound with left-hand *pizzicato*, his well-nigh incredible violinistic *tours de force*. To this end he made extensive use of variation forms. The Paganini variations on "God Save the King", his *Non più mesta* variations from *Cenerentola*, the variations on *Là ci darem la mano*, and the famous *Carnaval de Venise*, illustrate the method he used to elaborate simpler compositions. As a rule his adaptations begin with a recitative, after which the theme is introduced, followed by variations designed to give him full opportunity to display all his technical resources and tricks. I say this without prejudice to such works as his *24 Caprices*—which Liszt and Brahms transcribed in part for the piano—for these will always remain a monument to Paganini's creative genius.

But virtuosity for its own sake did not long endure, and the virtuoso compositions whose technical brilliancy were their chief claim to distinction, were very soon superseded by compositions of more genuine musical value. Spohr, Vieuxtemps, Ernst, Wieniawski, set other and higher standards. Spohr's gift of melodic invention was genuine, and in his violin music, more even than in any other of his works, he found that the conditions of formal development were suited to his classic mode of thought and his nature, and he enriched the repertory of the violin with really noble works. Of these, his Eighth Violin Concerto, the celebrated "Vocal Scene", is unquestionably his finest work—one every real violinist should study because in it technique is always subordinated to musical thought. Then, too—and this applies generally to Spohr's other Concertos as well—his treatment of the instrument is absolutely lyric. The Spohr *Adagios*, for example, are wonderful in their soulful melodic character. But to play Spohr properly, the violinist must give himself up altogether to the spirit of his music, and he must not begrudge his compositions the big, broad tone their rendering calls for.

90

Spohr's *Sonatas*, for that is what his *Duos Concertants* written for the violin and piano or harp really are, are technically on a level with the Concertos, rarely beautiful in conception, and well worth knowing.

Vieuxtemps's Concertos—especially the fine one in A minor—and his brilliant bravura compositions are all rich in beautiful musical ideas besides being quintessentially virtuoso music. I do not see how the discriminating violinist can well exclude them from his repertory. Aside from the formidable passage work incidental to brilliancy, these compositions of Vieuxtemps's are woven with many lovely melodies of an intimate character, melodies which sing beautifully on the instrument, and are distinctive both in theme and development. And as for Wieniawski, his *Légende*, the *Faust* Fantasy, and his *Adagio élégiaque*, with its many octave passages, are all, for similar reasons, well worth knowing. His two Concertos, especially the one in D minor, are rich in original themes, and are well written and rich in effect.

Ernst, too, wrote for the virtuoso player. But, like Vieuxtemps and Wieniawski, his compositions have far more than mere technique to recommend them. His expressive *Elégie*, his incredibly difficult transcription of Schubert's *Erlkönig*, his *Otello* fantasy, no violinist can afford to ignore. His Concerto in F sharp minor, however, though written with grace and distinction, is hardly important enough, musically, to hold a place among the great outstanding concertos of violin literature.

But Spohr and Vieuxtemps, especially, of these violinist-composers I have mentioned, still hold an unchallenged place, for their works, each in their own way, are at the present time regarded as masterpieces of distinct schools of musical thought and interpretation.

But it was about the middle of the nineteenth century that a nobler, more artistic trend made itself plainly evident in the recital programmes of the really great virtuosi. The change was inspired, I am inclined to think, by Mendelssohn, and, after his death, by Schumann in Leipzig and Liszt in Weimar. Ferdinand David and Joachim were the first to make a breach in the approved and sanctioned violin programme of their time.

David, having resurrected Johann Sebastian Bach's Sonatas

for violin solo (one of which contains the famous Chaconne), rendered an invaluable service to all the generations of violinists present and to come, by editing and publishing them. He still further enriched the repertory of the violin with his editions of the great Italian violin masters of the seventeenth and eighteenth centuries. To David almost exclusively belongs the credit of opening wide the gate of the seventeenth century to virtuosi of his day, as well as to those of our own. Through his efforts so vast a store of rich musical materials was made accessible that violinists have been making full and deserved use of them ever since. For together with the Sonatas of Johann Sebastian Bach and those of Handel, David's contributions form the basis of every well-constructed violin programme.

Between 1870 and 1880 this tendency to play music of the highest quality before public audiences had grown so widespread and the value of this principle had been so extensively recognized, accepted and supported by the press in general and the musical press in particular, that the great virtuosi like Wieniawski and Sarasate—the most conspicuous exponents of the movement—were encouraged to make extensive use of the higher type of violin composition in their concerts. With the most pronounced individuality of interpretation—I mean individuality in the best sense of the word—they included Bach's Chaconne and other of his compositions, as well as the Beethoven Concerto, on their programmes, and their very artistic conception of the adequate execution of these compositions added not a little to their fame. Sarasate's own original, ingenious and effective concert pieces, his *Airs Espagnols*, so warmly coloured with the fire and romance of his native land, are by no means his greatest tribute to the violin repertory. It was the wider appreciation he won by his playing of the great violin works of his own epoch for which he deserves the highest credit. To Sarasate belongs the distinction of having been the first to popularize the Concertos of Max Bruch, of Lalo and of Saint Saëns.

But as time went by, and the number of virtuosi was augmented year by year, increasing far more rapidly than the repertory itself, an effort was made to supply the demand for works worth while playing. Compositions were produced which not only had real musical value, but which pleased because of the manner in which they threw into relief the brilliant qualities of the solo instrument, as well as the virtuoso ability of the artist. The era of transcriptions, of arrangements of compositions, vocal or instrumental, which lent themselves more or less naturally to transfer to the strings, set in. The music of ancient and modern masters was made to contribute to this end.

The idea in itself was not new. Liszt had been the first to write transcriptions—those incomparable transcriptions of his for the piano. He introduced a new type of music for the keyboard and it is due to his genius that a number of vocal, violin, orchestral, etc., masterworks were made more generally accessible through his setting them down for the piano.

Joachim, in a modest way, and after him, Wilhelmj, more extensively, followed Liszt's example and were followed in turn by others. More than fifty years ago I myself transcribed Schubert's *Moments Musicaux* and Rubinstein's "Melody in F"; and edited Paganini's "Twenty-fourth Caprice"—the one in A minor —together with other similar compositions, with piano or other accompaniment.

Willy Burmeister, also a Joachim pupil, has during the past twenty years edited a number of smaller violin pieces taken from the works of the older masters, some of which have become very popular, and are still much played because of their intrinsic worth and the musicianship displayed in their presentation.

Later, Fritz Kreisler published his own admirable arrangements, as well as arrangements of some of Paganini's works, and he has been followed by Elman, Zimbalist and still others. It is thus that the standard repertory—the repertory which embraces the great concertos from Beethoven to Tchaikovsky, the Bach Sonatas, and the larger and more important individual violin pieces by all the good composers of older and more modern times —has been extended and, in a certain sense, renewed. For a host of charming and interesting pieces, if not originally violin music, have in many cases been made so, because their ideas have been "violinized", thought out again and expressed in the real musical and technical idiom of the string instrument.

And while he is awaiting the coming of the Johannes Brahms, Max Bruchs, Camille Saint-Saëns and the Tchaikovskys to be, the young virtuoso should not fail to take advantage of this new "miniature" repertory which, for many reasons, is so well worth cultivating.

But in the matter of developing a repertory, appropriate both in technique and temperament to the requirements of the young artist, what sort of music may we recommend as best suited to his taste and needs? Because it is so largely an individual matter, I find it difficult to be explicit. That the repertory have a wide range is one of the first essentials. I believe that he should vary, as widely as he possibly can, the music he plays. He ought to play the works of many different masters, and pass from a composition of one school to the work of a composer of an altogether different school. For the accomplished violinist must be musically broad: he must be at home in all the schools and know the repertory of each.

And this versatility applies as well to the study and exercise repertory for the technique of right and left hand as to the concert repertory. The student must master every form of technique; he must develop his mechanical faculties in every direction, just as far as the physical limitations of his hands will allow.

The range of compositions adapted to the young violinist's use is wide. Let him play whatever he likes by Bach, Beethoven and Mozart, while he makes himself familiar with the music of Schumann, Brahms and the moderns, or even dips into the purely virtuoso repertory. To develop good judgment in the selection of one's repertory is a difficult task, and many violinistic failures have been due to a lack of judgment in choosing the musical material to be studied. The young artist may easily be led astray unless controlled by genuine friends, whose judgment is reliable. If he does not have the benefit of such guidance it is only too likely that his errors will be brought home to him rather late in the day by severe criticism.

But as soon as the student has reached a certain maturity both of age and of judgment, when he has overcome many of his early faults—whether this be as a result of the advice of teachers, of colleagues or of friends—he will feel the need of, and tend to rely more and more upon self-criticism and self-analysis. He will sound, study, examine his equipment, musical and technical, his taste, his preferences, his temperament, and he will be guided in his choice of numbers to be added to his repertory by a proper balance of such factors and a recognition of his own limitations and abilities. In this way the whole question of repertory will gradually solve itself for him, for repertory—aside from the acknowledgedly great works which he must study, know and play if he is to be considered, in any true sense of the word, a violinist—should mean those compositions which each individual violinist can play to best advantage, which he best feels and interprets, and his own instinct and judgment must be his ultimate guide in this. The music which speaks most powerfully to his own soul he will be able to present most sincerely, most appealingly, to his listeners. Let him set himself this standard, and live up to it, and his repertory will take care of itself.

In trying to develop his own sense of what a repertory should be, the student ought to neglect no opportunity of hearing violinists, always listening intelligently to what they play, and trying to study the effect of the music played. He will do well to hear mediocre players as well as the great artists. From the former he can learn what *not* to play and how *not* to play; while the latter will teach him what is worth knowing and its interpretation. Yet, in every case, he must remember that while he should learn all he possibly can from these artists, he must never imitate them.

I have always developed the repertory of my pupils on broad lines of general appreciation and individual preference. The best of all schools, the best of all types, the music best adapted to the character and powers of the individual—this makes up the repertory of the true artist violinist.

CHAPTER XIV

PRACTICAL REPERTORY HINTS

WHAT I GIVE MY PUPILS TO PLAY

I BELIEVE that, in order to maintain the student's interest in his work, a competent violin teacher will make use of teaching material of as widely varied a character as possible, and that he will under no circumstances concentrate on the works of any one composer, no matter how important, to the exclusion of others. I have always acted on this conviction in the case of my own pupils.

After working his way through Kreutzer's forty *Etudes* and the twenty-four *Caprices* by Rode, the young violinist may take up such compositions as the Viotti Concerto in A minor, or that in E minor by the same composer; Rode's two Concertos in A minor and E minor are also very valuable; the D minor and D major Concertos of Kreutzer, and Spohr's Second Concerto, in D minor, and at the same time and at certain intervals, such pieces as Vieuxtemps's *Rêverie*, the *Morceau de Salon* in D minor, the *Ballade et Polonaise*, the *Tarantelle* in A minor—unjustly neglected—and, later, the big *Fantasie Appassionata*, as well as other, shorter compositions of a more singing character.

Afterwards, when the student has completed the Rode *Etudes* and those of Rovelli, and has started work on Jacques Dont's twenty-four *Caprices*, he may try his hand at more difficult concertos: Spohr's No. 7, and his No. 8, the "Vocal Scena", as well as the Concerto No. 9, in D minor, and the one in G major, No. 11. But the study of all these concertos should be varied and enlivened by the introduction of other less difficult things: pieces by Wieniawski, such as the *Légende*, some of the mazurkas, one of the two *Polonaises*, the one in A, for instance, to begin with, since it is the easier of the two. And the student may also take up one of the two books of Sarasate's *Danses Espagnoles*, not forgetting to pay attention to the slow movements which occur in them; and one or another of the Chopin *Nocturnes*, of which Sarasate, Wilhelmj and I myself have made transcriptions.

After the student has mastered Rode's twenty-four *Caprices*, and the *Caprices* by Dont—I mean "mastered", not as a result of running through from beginning to end in a superficial manner, but of studying them with the most serious devotion, and devoting special attention to some of the more individual and difficult ones among them—then he may venture upon some of the works of the grand repertory: the Concertos of Mendelssohn, Beethoven, Brahms, Tchaikovsky, together with movements taken from Bach's Six Sonatas for violin solo,[1] and the two Beethoven Romances, as well as more modern compositions. Of these latter there are many which are worth while studying: some of the arrangements which Kreisler has made of numbers by older masters; my own transcriptions of pieces by Beethoven, Schumann, Tchaikovsky; Ries's *Troisième Suite*; the more recent transcriptions of numbers by Grieg, Rubinstein, Fauré and others made by Mischa Elman; Zimbalist's *Danses Orientales* and his *Suite dans le style ancien*; the "Hebrew Melody" and "Hebrew Lullaby" by Achron.

Then come such works as Tartini's two Sonatas—the one in G minor and "The Devil's Trill" Sonata—various other sonatas by the older Italian masters, and the Vieuxtemps Concertos—No. 2, in F sharp minor, No. 4, in D minor, No. 1, in E major, and No. 5, in A minor. The sequence of these Vieuxtemps Concertos may be broken up by Wieniawski's Concerto No. 2, in D minor, Ernst's *Fantasie brillante* on themes from "Otello", and the *Airs hongrois* by the same composer; Wieniawski's Concerto in F sharp minor; the Ernst F sharp minor Concerto, and Paganini's Concerto in D major.

This last group of compositions represents the very maximum of technical difficulty, and should be diversified by *cantabile* numbers, violin-song numbers, like the Bach-Wilhelmj *Air* on the G-string; Handel's *Larghetto*, as arranged by Eddy Brown, and

[1] With regard to J. S. Bach's two Concertos for violin, I have never given them to my pupils to study because, from my point of view, only the two slow movements in them are musically valuable and really worthy of their composer; while the first and last movements of each Concerto are not very interesting, either musically or technically. This, of course, is my own humble opinion.

three or four of the Handel Sonatas, especially those in E, A and D major. I have mentioned elsewhere the Concertos of Max Bruch and Saint-Saëns, and the *Symphonie Espagnole* by Lalo, which, of course, must be included in the study programme of every solo violinist as permanent features of the virtuoso repertory of our own time.

These numbers here mentioned are all compositions which I have studied myself, and which I make my pupils study.

Nor should I neglect some of the Paganini compositions I have not touched on elsewhere, which I have found most valuable for study purposes because of their effect as concert numbers. Among them is the twenty-fourth *Caprice*, in A minor, for which I have supplied a piano accompaniment, and the famous *Perpetuum mobile* (Perpetual Motion), one of the most difficult compositions ever written as far as bow technique is concerned.

Once the young artist has really mastered the repertory whose components I have indicated in a broad way, he will have attained a notable degree of mechanical skill and musical sufficiency. And his taste, moreover—thanks to the large number of works diverse in character and rich in musical beauty which he will have come to know—will have been formed. He will then be perfectly justified in developing a repertory for himself in accordance with *his* preferences conformable to *his* capacities, extending or reducing the one I have described, and substituting for the works mentioned others which represent his own choice.

In giving these indications of the *études* and concertos which I have been in the habit of using in my courses at the Imperial Conservatory in Petrograd and in the United States, I do not mean to insist that they be followed out in the exact order in which they are given. It goes almost without saying that I have not here set down my conclusions as hard and fast rules for the study of repertory. They are suggestive rather than positive, and it is of slight importance if the sequence of study indicated be varied, according as the teacher's insight or the student's individuality may justify departures from the order given.

Like all else that pertains to art, though an order of succession for the study of repertory may be planned on certain principles based on generally accepted laws, it is the individual factor which must be the determining one in the end. Intuition, instinct, physical equipment, and intellectual bias eventually lay down the law, and what, for want of a better term, we know as "genius" will—even when opposed—continue to dominate and control in the present and in the future precisely as it has in the past.

A CATALOG OF SELECTED
DOVER BOOKS
IN ALL FIELDS OF INTEREST

A CATALOG OF SELECTED DOVER BOOKS IN ALL FIELDS OF INTEREST

CONCERNING THE SPIRITUAL IN ART, Wassily Kandinsky. Pioneering work by father of abstract art. Thoughts on color theory, nature of art. Analysis of earlier masters. 12 illustrations. 80pp. of text. 5⅜ x 8½. 23411-8

ANIMALS: 1,419 Copyright-Free Illustrations of Mammals, Birds, Fish, Insects, etc., Jim Harter (ed.). Clear wood engravings present, in extremely lifelike poses, over 1,000 species of animals. One of the most extensive pictorial sourcebooks of its kind. Captions. Index. 284pp. 9 x 12. 23766-4

CELTIC ART: The Methods of Construction, George Bain. Simple geometric techniques for making Celtic interlacements, spirals, Kells-type initials, animals, humans, etc. Over 500 illustrations. 160pp. 9 x 12. (Available in U.S. only.) 22923-8

AN ATLAS OF ANATOMY FOR ARTISTS, Fritz Schider. Most thorough reference work on art anatomy in the world. Hundreds of illustrations, including selections from works by Vesalius, Leonardo, Goya, Ingres, Michelangelo, others. 593 illustrations. 192pp. 7⅛ x 10¼. 20241-0

CELTIC HAND STROKE-BY-STROKE (Irish Half-Uncial from "The Book of Kells"): An Arthur Baker Calligraphy Manual, Arthur Baker. Complete guide to creating each letter of the alphabet in distinctive Celtic manner. Covers hand position, strokes, pens, inks, paper, more. Illustrated. 48pp. 8¼ x 11. 24336-2

EASY ORIGAMI, John Montroll. Charming collection of 32 projects (hat, cup, pelican, piano, swan, many more) specially designed for the novice origami hobbyist. Clearly illustrated easy-to-follow instructions insure that even beginning papercrafters will achieve successful results. 48pp. 8¼ x 11. 27298-2

THE COMPLETE BOOK OF BIRDHOUSE CONSTRUCTION FOR WOOD-WORKERS, Scott D. Campbell. Detailed instructions, illustrations, tables. Also data on bird habitat and instinct patterns. Bibliography. 3 tables. 63 illustrations in 15 figures. 48pp. 5¼ x 8½. 24407-5

BLOOMINGDALE'S ILLUSTRATED 1886 CATALOG: Fashions, Dry Goods and Housewares, Bloomingdale Brothers. Famed merchants' extremely rare catalog depicting about 1,700 products: clothing, housewares, firearms, dry goods, jewelry, more. Invaluable for dating, identifying vintage items. Also, copyright-free graphics for artists, designers. Co-published with Henry Ford Museum & Greenfield Village. 160pp. 8¼ x 11. 25780-0

HISTORIC COSTUME IN PICTURES, Braun & Schneider. Over 1,450 costumed figures in clearly detailed engravings–from dawn of civilization to end of 19th century. Captions. Many folk costumes. 256pp. 8⅜ x 11¾. 23150-X

HOLLYWOOD GLAMOR PORTRAITS, John Kobal (ed.). 145 photos from 1926-49. Harlow, Gable, Bogart, Bacall; 94 stars in all. Full background on photographers, technical aspects. 160pp. 8⅜ x 11¼.   23352-9

FRANK LLOYD WRIGHT'S DANA HOUSE, Donald Hoffmann. Pictorial essay of residential masterpiece with over 160 interior and exterior photos, plans, elevations, sketches and studies. 128pp. 9¼ x 10¾.   29120-0

THE MALE AND FEMALE FIGURE IN MOTION: 60 Classic Photographic Sequences, Eadweard Muybridge. 60 true-action photographs of men and women walking, running, climbing, bending, turning, etc., reproduced from rare 19th-century masterpiece. vi + 121pp. 9 x 12.   24745-7

1001 QUESTIONS ANSWERED ABOUT THE SEASHORE, N. J. Berrill and Jacquelyn Berrill. Queries answered about dolphins, sea snails, sponges, starfish, fishes, shore birds, many others. Covers appearance, breeding, growth, feeding, much more. 305pp. 5¼ x 8¼.   23366-9

ATTRACTING BIRDS TO YOUR YARD, William J. Weber. Easy-to-follow guide offers advice on how to attract the greatest diversity of birds: birdhouses, feeders, water and waterers, much more. 96pp. 5³⁄₁₆ x 8¼.   28927-3

MEDICINAL AND OTHER USES OF NORTH AMERICAN PLANTS: A Historical Survey with Special Reference to the Eastern Indian Tribes, Charlotte Erichsen-Brown. Chronological historical citations document 500 years of usage of plants, trees, shrubs native to eastern Canada, northeastern U.S. Also complete identifying information. 343 illustrations. 544pp. 6½ x 9¼.   25951-X

STORYBOOK MAZES, Dave Phillips. 23 stories and mazes on two-page spreads: Wizard of Oz, Treasure Island, Robin Hood, etc. Solutions. 64pp. 8¼ x 11.   23628-5

AMERICAN NEGRO SONGS: 230 Folk Songs and Spirituals, Religious and Secular, John W. Work. This authoritative study traces the African influences of songs sung and played by black Americans at work, in church, and as entertainment. The author discusses the lyric significance of such songs as "Swing Low, Sweet Chariot," "John Henry," and others and offers the words and music for 230 songs. Bibliography. Index of Song Titles. 272pp. 6½ x 9¼.   40271-1

MOVIE-STAR PORTRAITS OF THE FORTIES, John Kobal (ed.). 163 glamor, studio photos of 106 stars of the 1940s: Rita Hayworth, Ava Gardner, Marlon Brando, Clark Gable, many more. 176pp. 8⅜ x 11¼.   23546-7

BENCHLEY LOST AND FOUND, Robert Benchley. Finest humor from early 30s, about pet peeves, child psychologists, post office and others. Mostly unavailable elsewhere. 73 illustrations by Peter Arno and others. 183pp. 5⅜ x 8½.   22410-4

YEKL and THE IMPORTED BRIDEGROOM AND OTHER STORIES OF YIDDISH NEW YORK, Abraham Cahan. Film Hester Street based on *Yekl* (1896). Novel, other stories among first about Jewish immigrants on N.Y.'s East Side. 240pp. 5⅜ x 8½.   22427-9

SELECTED POEMS, Walt Whitman. Generous sampling from *Leaves of Grass*. Twenty-four poems include "I Hear America Singing," "Song of the Open Road," "I Sing the Body Electric," "When Lilacs Last in the Dooryard Bloom'd," "O Captain! My Captain!"—all reprinted from an authoritative edition. Lists of titles and first lines. 128pp. 5³⁄₁₆ x 8¼.   26878-0

THE BEST TALES OF HOFFMANN, E. T. A. Hoffmann. 10 of Hoffmann's most important stories: "Nutcracker and the King of Mice," "The Golden Flowerpot," etc. 458pp. 5⅜ x 8½. 21793-0

FROM FETISH TO GOD IN ANCIENT EGYPT, E. A. Wallis Budge. Rich detailed survey of Egyptian conception of "God" and gods, magic, cult of animals, Osiris, more. Also, superb English translations of hymns and legends. 240 illustrations. 545pp. 5⅜ x 8½. 25803-3

FRENCH STORIES/CONTES FRANÇAIS: A Dual-Language Book, Wallace Fowlie. Ten stories by French masters, Voltaire to Camus: "Micromegas" by Voltaire; "The Atheist's Mass" by Balzac; "Minuet" by de Maupassant; "The Guest" by Camus, six more. Excellent English translations on facing pages. Also French-English vocabulary list, exercises, more. 352pp. 5⅜ x 8½. 26443-2

CHICAGO AT THE TURN OF THE CENTURY IN PHOTOGRAPHS: 122 Historic Views from the Collections of the Chicago Historical Society, Larry A. Viskochil. Rare large-format prints offer detailed views of City Hall, State Street, the Loop, Hull House, Union Station, many other landmarks, circa 1904-1913. Introduction. Captions. Maps. 144pp. 9⅜ x 12¼. 24656-6

OLD BROOKLYN IN EARLY PHOTOGRAPHS, 1865-1929, William Lee Younger. Luna Park, Gravesend race track, construction of Grand Army Plaza, moving of Hotel Brighton, etc. 157 previously unpublished photographs. 165pp. 8⅞ x 11¾. 23587-4

THE MYTHS OF THE NORTH AMERICAN INDIANS, Lewis Spence. Rich anthology of the myths and legends of the Algonquins, Iroquois, Pawnees and Sioux, prefaced by an extensive historical and ethnological commentary. 36 illustrations. 480pp. 5⅜ x 8½. 25967-6

AN ENCYCLOPEDIA OF BATTLES: Accounts of Over 1,560 Battles from 1479 B.C. to the Present, David Eggenberger. Essential details of every major battle in recorded history from the first battle of Megiddo in 1479 B.C. to Grenada in 1984. List of Battle Maps. New Appendix covering the years 1967-1984. Index. 99 illustrations. 544pp. 6½ x 9¼. 24913-1

SAILING ALONE AROUND THE WORLD, Captain Joshua Slocum. First man to sail around the world, alone, in small boat. One of great feats of seamanship told in delightful manner. 67 illustrations. 294pp. 5⅜ x 8½. 20326-3

ANARCHISM AND OTHER ESSAYS, Emma Goldman. Powerful, penetrating, prophetic essays on direct action, role of minorities, prison reform, puritan hypocrisy, violence, etc. 271pp. 5⅜ x 8½. 22484-8

MYTHS OF THE HINDUS AND BUDDHISTS, Ananda K. Coomaraswamy and Sister Nivedita. Great stories of the epics; deeds of Krishna, Shiva, taken from puranas, Vedas, folk tales; etc. 32 illustrations. 400pp. 5⅜ x 8½. 21759-0

THE TRAUMA OF BIRTH, Otto Rank. Rank's controversial thesis that anxiety neurosis is caused by profound psychological trauma which occurs at birth. 256pp. 5¾ x 8½. 27974-X

A THEOLOGICO-POLITICAL TREATISE, Benedict Spinoza. Also contains unfinished Political Treatise. Great classic on religious liberty, theory of government on common consent. R. Elwes translation. Total of 421pp. 5⅜ x 8½. 20249-6

MY BONDAGE AND MY FREEDOM, Frederick Douglass. Born a slave, Douglass became outspoken force in antislavery movement. The best of Douglass' autobiographies. Graphic description of slave life. 464pp. 5⅜ x 8½.   22457-0

FOLLOWING THE EQUATOR: A Journey Around the World, Mark Twain. Fascinating humorous account of 1897 voyage to Hawaii, Australia, India, New Zealand, etc. Ironic, bemused reports on peoples, customs, climate, flora and fauna, politics, much more. 197 illustrations. 720pp. 5⅜ x 8½.   26113-1

THE PEOPLE CALLED SHAKERS, Edward D. Andrews. Definitive study of Shakers: origins, beliefs, practices, dances, social organization, furniture and crafts, etc. 33 illustrations. 351pp. 5⅜ x 8½.   21081-2

THE MYTHS OF GREECE AND ROME, H. A. Guerber. A classic of mythology, generously illustrated, long prized for its simple, graphic, accurate retelling of the principal myths of Greece and Rome, and for its commentary on their origins and significance. With 64 illustrations by Michelangelo, Raphael, Titian, Rubens, Canova, Bernini and others. 480pp. 5⅜ x 8½.   27584-1

PSYCHOLOGY OF MUSIC, Carl E. Seashore. Classic work discusses music as a medium from psychological viewpoint. Clear treatment of physical acoustics, auditory apparatus, sound perception, development of musical skills, nature of musical feeling, host of other topics. 88 figures. 408pp. 5⅜ x 8½.   21851-1

THE PHILOSOPHY OF HISTORY, Georg W. Hegel. Great classic of Western thought develops concept that history is not chance but rational process, the evolution of freedom. 457pp. 5⅜ x 8½.   20112-0

THE BOOK OF TEA, Kakuzo Okakura. Minor classic of the Orient: entertaining, charming explanation, interpretation of traditional Japanese culture in terms of tea ceremony. 94pp. 5⅜ x 8½.   20070-1

LIFE IN ANCIENT EGYPT, Adolf Erman. Fullest, most thorough, detailed older account with much not in more recent books, domestic life, religion, magic, medicine, commerce, much more. Many illustrations reproduce tomb paintings, carvings, hieroglyphs, etc. 597pp. 5⅜ x 8½.   22632-8

SUNDIALS, Their Theory and Construction, Albert Waugh. Far and away the best, most thorough coverage of ideas, mathematics concerned, types, construction, adjusting anywhere. Simple, nontechnical treatment allows even children to build several of these dials. Over 100 illustrations. 230pp. 5⅜ x 8½.   22947-5

THEORETICAL HYDRODYNAMICS, L. M. Milne-Thomson. Classic exposition of the mathematical theory of fluid motion, applicable to both hydrodynamics and aerodynamics. Over 600 exercises. 768pp. 6⅛ x 9¼.   68970-0

SONGS OF EXPERIENCE: Facsimile Reproduction with 26 Plates in Full Color, William Blake. 26 full-color plates from a rare 1826 edition. Includes "The Tyger," "London," "Holy Thursday," and other poems. Printed text of poems. 48pp. 5¼ x 7.
24636-1

OLD-TIME VIGNETTES IN FULL COLOR, Carol Belanger Grafton (ed.). Over 390 charming, often sentimental illustrations, selected from archives of Victorian graphics—pretty women posing, children playing, food, flowers, kittens and puppies, smiling cherubs, birds and butterflies, much more. All copyright-free. 48pp. 9¼ x 12¼.
27269-9

PERSPECTIVE FOR ARTISTS, Rex Vicat Cole. Depth, perspective of sky and sea, shadows, much more, not usually covered. 391 diagrams, 81 reproductions of drawings and paintings. 279pp. 5⅜ x 8½. 22487-2

DRAWING THE LIVING FIGURE, Joseph Sheppard. Innovative approach to artistic anatomy focuses on specifics of surface anatomy, rather than muscles and bones. Over 170 drawings of live models in front, back and side views, and in widely varying poses. Accompanying diagrams. 177 illustrations. Introduction. Index. 144pp. 8⅜ x11¼. 26723-7

GOTHIC AND OLD ENGLISH ALPHABETS: 100 Complete Fonts, Dan X. Solo. Add power, elegance to posters, signs, other graphics with 100 stunning copyright-free alphabets: Blackstone, Dolbey, Germania, 97 more–including many lower-case, numerals, punctuation marks. 104pp. 8⅛ x 11. 24695-7

HOW TO DO BEADWORK, Mary White. Fundamental book on craft from simple projects to five-bead chains and woven works. 106 illustrations. 142pp. 5⅜ x 8. 20697-1

THE BOOK OF WOOD CARVING, Charles Marshall Sayers. Finest book for beginners discusses fundamentals and offers 34 designs. "Absolutely first rate . . . well thought out and well executed."–E. J. Tangerman. 118pp. 7¾ x 10⅝. 23654-4

ILLUSTRATED CATALOG OF CIVIL WAR MILITARY GOODS: Union Army Weapons, Insignia, Uniform Accessories, and Other Equipment, Schuyler, Hartley, and Graham. Rare, profusely illustrated 1846 catalog includes Union Army uniform and dress regulations, arms and ammunition, coats, insignia, flags, swords, rifles, etc. 226 illustrations. 160pp. 9 x 12. 24939-5

WOMEN'S FASHIONS OF THE EARLY 1900s: An Unabridged Republication of "New York Fashions, 1909," National Cloak & Suit Co. Rare catalog of mail-order fashions documents women's and children's clothing styles shortly after the turn of the century. Captions offer full descriptions, prices. Invaluable resource for fashion, costume historians. Approximately 725 illustrations. 128pp. 8⅜ x 11¼. 27276-1

THE 1912 AND 1915 GUSTAV STICKLEY FURNITURE CATALOGS, Gustav Stickley. With over 200 detailed illustrations and descriptions, these two catalogs are essential reading and reference materials and identification guides for Stickley furniture. Captions cite materials, dimensions and prices. 112pp. 6½ x 9¼. 26676-1

EARLY AMERICAN LOCOMOTIVES, John H. White, Jr. Finest locomotive engravings from early 19th century: historical (1804–74), main-line (after 1870), special, foreign, etc. 147 plates. 142pp. 11⅜ x 8¼. 22772-3

THE TALL SHIPS OF TODAY IN PHOTOGRAPHS, Frank O. Braynard. Lavishly illustrated tribute to nearly 100 majestic contemporary sailing vessels: Amerigo Vespucci, Clearwater, Constitution, Eagle, Mayflower, Sea Cloud, Victory, many more. Authoritative captions provide statistics, background on each ship. 190 black-and-white photographs and illustrations. Introduction. 128pp. 8⅞ x 11¾. 27163-3

LITTLE BOOK OF EARLY AMERICAN CRAFTS AND TRADES, Peter Stockham (ed.). 1807 children's book explains crafts and trades: baker, hatter, cooper, potter, and many others. 23 copperplate illustrations. 140pp. 4⅝ x 6. 23336-7

VICTORIAN FASHIONS AND COSTUMES FROM HARPER'S BAZAR, 1867–1898, Stella Blum (ed.). Day costumes, evening wear, sports clothes, shoes, hats, other accessories in over 1,000 detailed engravings. 320pp. 9⅜ x 12¼. 22990-4

GUSTAV STICKLEY, THE CRAFTSMAN, Mary Ann Smith. Superb study surveys broad scope of Stickley's achievement, especially in architecture. Design philosophy, rise and fall of the Craftsman empire, descriptions and floor plans for many Craftsman houses, more. 86 black-and-white halftones. 31 line illustrations. Introduction 208pp. 6½ x 9¼. 27210-9

THE LONG ISLAND RAIL ROAD IN EARLY PHOTOGRAPHS, Ron Ziel. Over 220 rare photos, informative text document origin (1844) and development of rail service on Long Island. Vintage views of early trains, locomotives, stations, passengers, crews, much more. Captions. 8⅞ x 11¾. 26301-0

VOYAGE OF THE LIBERDADE, Joshua Slocum. Great 19th-century mariner's thrilling, first-hand account of the wreck of his ship off South America, the 35-foot boat he built from the wreckage, and its remarkable voyage home. 128pp. 5⅜ x 8½. 40022-0

TEN BOOKS ON ARCHITECTURE, Vitruvius. The most important book ever written on architecture. Early Roman aesthetics, technology, classical orders, site selection, all other aspects. Morgan translation. 331pp. 5⅜ x 8½. 20645-9

THE HUMAN FIGURE IN MOTION, Eadweard Muybridge. More than 4,500 stopped-action photos, in action series, showing undraped men, women, children jumping, lying down, throwing, sitting, wrestling, carrying, etc. 390pp. 7⅞ x 10⅝. 20204-6 Clothbd.

TREES OF THE EASTERN AND CENTRAL UNITED STATES AND CANADA, William M. Harlow. Best one-volume guide to 140 trees. Full descriptions, woodlore, range, etc. Over 600 illustrations. Handy size. 288pp. 4½ x 6⅜. 20395-6

SONGS OF WESTERN BIRDS, Dr. Donald J. Borror. Complete song and call repertoire of 60 western species, including flycatchers, juncoes, cactus wrens, many more–includes fully illustrated booklet. Cassette and manual 99913-0

GROWING AND USING HERBS AND SPICES, Milo Miloradovich. Versatile handbook provides all the information needed for cultivation and use of all the herbs and spices available in North America. 4 illustrations. Index. Glossary. 236pp. 5⅜ x 8½. 25058-X

BIG BOOK OF MAZES AND LABYRINTHS, Walter Shepherd. 50 mazes and labyrinths in all–classical, solid, ripple, and more–in one great volume. Perfect inexpensive puzzler for clever youngsters. Full solutions. 112pp. 8⅛ x 11. 22951-3

PIANO TUNING, J. Cree Fischer. Clearest, best book for beginner, amateur. Simple repairs, raising dropped notes, tuning by easy method of flattened fifths. No previous skills needed. 4 illustrations. 201pp. 5⅜ x 8½. 23267-0

HINTS TO SINGERS, Lillian Nordica. Selecting the right teacher, developing confidence, overcoming stage fright, and many other important skills receive thoughtful discussion in this indispensible guide, written by a world-famous diva of four decades' experience. 96pp. 5⅜ x 8½. 40094-8

THE COMPLETE NONSENSE OF EDWARD LEAR, Edward Lear. All nonsense limericks, zany alphabets, Owl and Pussycat, songs, nonsense botany, etc., illustrated by Lear. Total of 320pp. 5⅜ x 8½. (Available in U.S. only.) 20167-8

VICTORIAN PARLOUR POETRY: An Annotated Anthology, Michael R. Turner. 117 gems by Longfellow, Tennyson, Browning, many lesser-known poets. "The Village Blacksmith," "Curfew Must Not Ring Tonight," "Only a Baby Small," dozens more, often difficult to find elsewhere. Index of poets, titles, first lines. xxiii + 325pp. 5⅝ x 8¼. 27044-0

DUBLINERS, James Joyce. Fifteen stories offer vivid, tightly focused observations of the lives of Dublin's poorer classes. At least one, "The Dead," is considered a masterpiece. Reprinted complete and unabridged from standard edition. 160pp. 5³⁄₁₆ x 8¼. 26870-5

GREAT WEIRD TALES: 14 Stories by Lovecraft, Blackwood, Machen and Others, S. T. Joshi (ed.). 14 spellbinding tales, including "The Sin Eater," by Fiona McLeod, "The Eye Above the Mantel," by Frank Belknap Long, as well as renowned works by R. H. Barlow, Lord Dunsany, Arthur Machen, W. C. Morrow and eight other masters of the genre. 256pp. 5⅜ x 8½. (Available in U.S. only.) 40436-6

THE BOOK OF THE SACRED MAGIC OF ABRAMELIN THE MAGE, translated by S. MacGregor Mathers. Medieval manuscript of ceremonial magic. Basic document in Aleister Crowley, Golden Dawn groups. 268pp. 5⅜ x 8½. 23211-5

NEW RUSSIAN-ENGLISH AND ENGLISH-RUSSIAN DICTIONARY, M. A. O'Brien. This is a remarkably handy Russian dictionary, containing a surprising amount of information, including over 70,000 entries. 366pp. 4½ x 6⅛. 20208-9

HISTORIC HOMES OF THE AMERICAN PRESIDENTS, Second, Revised Edition, Irvin Haas. A traveler's guide to American Presidential homes, most open to the public, depicting and describing homes occupied by every American President from George Washington to George Bush. With visiting hours, admission charges, travel routes. 175 photographs. Index. 160pp. 8¼ x 11. 26751-2

NEW YORK IN THE FORTIES, Andreas Feininger. 162 brilliant photographs by the well-known photographer, formerly with *Life* magazine. Commuters, shoppers, Times Square at night, much else from city at its peak. Captions by John von Hartz. 181pp. 9¼ x 10¾. 23585-8

INDIAN SIGN LANGUAGE, William Tomkins. Over 525 signs developed by Sioux and other tribes. Written instructions and diagrams. Also 290 pictographs. 111pp. 6⅛ x 9¼. 22029-X

ANATOMY: A Complete Guide for Artists, Joseph Sheppard. A master of figure drawing shows artists how to render human anatomy convincingly. Over 460 illustrations. 224pp. 8⅜ x 11¼. 27279-6

MEDIEVAL CALLIGRAPHY: Its History and Technique, Marc Drogin. Spirited history, comprehensive instruction manual covers 13 styles (ca. 4th century through 15th). Excellent photographs; directions for duplicating medieval techniques with modern tools. 224pp. 8⅜ x 11¼. 26142-5

DRIED FLOWERS: How to Prepare Them, Sarah Whitlock and Martha Rankin. Complete instructions on how to use silica gel, meal and borax, perlite aggregate, sand and borax, glycerine and water to create attractive permanent flower arrangements. 12 illustrations. 32pp. 5⅜ x 8½. 21802-3

EASY-TO-MAKE BIRD FEEDERS FOR WOODWORKERS, Scott D. Campbell. Detailed, simple-to-use guide for designing, constructing, caring for and using feeders. Text, illustrations for 12 classic and contemporary designs. 96pp. 5⅜ x 8½.
25847-5

SCOTTISH WONDER TALES FROM MYTH AND LEGEND, Donald A. Mackenzie. 16 lively tales tell of giants rumbling down mountainsides, of a magic wand that turns stone pillars into warriors, of gods and goddesses, evil hags, powerful forces and more. 240pp. 5⅜ x 8½. 29677-6

THE HISTORY OF UNDERCLOTHES, C. Willett Cunnington and Phyllis Cunnington. Fascinating, well-documented survey covering six centuries of English undergarments, enhanced with over 100 illustrations: 12th-century laced-up bodice, footed long drawers (1795), 19th-century bustles, 19th-century corsets for men, Victorian "bust improvers," much more. 272pp. 5⅜ x 8¼. 27124-2

ARTS AND CRAFTS FURNITURE: The Complete Brooks Catalog of 1912, Brooks Manufacturing Co. Photos and detailed descriptions of more than 150 now very collectible furniture designs from the Arts and Crafts movement depict davenports, settees, buffets, desks, tables, chairs, bedsteads, dressers and more, all built of solid, quarter-sawed oak. Invaluable for students and enthusiasts of antiques, Americana and the decorative arts. 80pp. 6½ x 9¼. 27471-3

WILBUR AND ORVILLE: A Biography of the Wright Brothers, Fred Howard. Definitive, crisply written study tells the full story of the brothers' lives and work. A vividly written biography, unparalleled in scope and color, that also captures the spirit of an extraordinary era. 560pp. 6⅛ x 9¼. 40297-5

THE ARTS OF THE SAILOR: Knotting, Splicing and Ropework, Hervey Garrett Smith. Indispensable shipboard reference covers tools, basic knots and useful hitches; handsewing and canvas work, more. Over 100 illustrations. Delightful reading for sea lovers. 256pp. 5⅜ x 8½. 26440-8

FRANK LLOYD WRIGHT'S FALLINGWATER: The House and Its History, Second, Revised Edition, Donald Hoffmann. A total revision–both in text and illustrations–of the standard document on Fallingwater, the boldest, most personal architectural statement of Wright's mature years, updated with valuable new material from the recently opened Frank Lloyd Wright Archives. "Fascinating"–*The New York Times*. 116 illustrations. 128pp. 9¼ x 10¾. 27430-6

THE WIT AND HUMOR OF OSCAR WILDE, Alvin Redman (ed.). More than 1,000 ripostes, paradoxes, wisecracks: Work is the curse of the drinking classes; I can resist everything except temptation; etc. 258pp. 5⅜ x 8½. 20602-5

SHAKESPEARE LEXICON AND QUOTATION DICTIONARY, Alexander Schmidt. Full definitions, locations, shades of meaning in every word in plays and poems. More than 50,000 exact quotations. 1,485pp. 6½ x 9¼. 2-vol. set.

Vol. 1: 22726-X
Vol. 2: 22727-8

SELECTED POEMS, Emily Dickinson. Over 100 best-known, best-loved poems by one of America's foremost poets, reprinted from authoritative early editions. No comparable edition at this price. Index of first lines. 64pp. 5³⁄₁₆ x 8¼. 26466-1

THE INSIDIOUS DR. FU-MANCHU, Sax Rohmer. The first of the popular mystery series introduces a pair of English detectives to their archnemesis, the diabolical Dr. Fu-Manchu. Flavorful atmosphere, fast-paced action, and colorful characters enliven this classic of the genre. 208pp. 5³⁄₁₆ x 8¼. 29898-1

THE MALLEUS MALEFICARUM OF KRAMER AND SPRENGER, translated by Montague Summers. Full text of most important witchhunter's "bible," used by both Catholics and Protestants. 278pp. 6⅝ x 10. 22802-9

SPANISH STORIES/CUENTOS ESPAÑOLES: A Dual-Language Book, Angel Flores (ed.). Unique format offers 13 great stories in Spanish by Cervantes, Borges, others. Faithful English translations on facing pages. 352pp. 5⅜ x 8½. 25399-6

GARDEN CITY, LONG ISLAND, IN EARLY PHOTOGRAPHS, 1869–1919, Mildred H. Smith. Handsome treasury of 118 vintage pictures, accompanied by carefully researched captions, document the Garden City Hotel fire (1899), the Vanderbilt Cup Race (1908), the first airmail flight departing from the Nassau Boulevard Aerodrome (1911), and much more. 96pp. 8⅞ x 11¾. 40669-5

OLD QUEENS, N.Y., IN EARLY PHOTOGRAPHS, Vincent F. Seyfried and William Asadorian. Over 160 rare photographs of Maspeth, Jamaica, Jackson Heights, and other areas. Vintage views of DeWitt Clinton mansion, 1939 World's Fair and more. Captions. 192pp. 8⅞ x 11. 26358-4

CAPTURED BY THE INDIANS: 15 Firsthand Accounts, 1750-1870, Frederick Drimmer. Astounding true historical accounts of grisly torture, bloody conflicts, relentless pursuits, miraculous escapes and more, by people who lived to tell the tale. 384pp. 5⅜ x 8½. 24901-8

THE WORLD'S GREAT SPEECHES (Fourth Enlarged Edition), Lewis Copeland, Lawrence W. Lamm, and Stephen J. McKenna. Nearly 300 speeches provide public speakers with a wealth of updated quotes and inspiration—from Pericles' funeral oration and William Jennings Bryan's "Cross of Gold Speech" to Malcolm X's powerful words on the Black Revolution and Earl of Spenser's tribute to his sister, Diana, Princess of Wales. 944pp. 5⅜ x 8⅜. 40903-1

THE BOOK OF THE SWORD, Sir Richard F. Burton. Great Victorian scholar/adventurer's eloquent, erudite history of the "queen of weapons"—from prehistory to early Roman Empire. Evolution and development of early swords, variations (sabre, broadsword, cutlass, scimitar, etc.), much more. 336pp. 6⅛ x 9¼. 25434-8

THE STORY OF THE TITANIC AS TOLD BY ITS SURVIVORS, Jack Winocour (ed.). What it was really like. Panic, despair, shocking inefficiency, and a little hero-ism. More thrilling than any fictional account. 26 illustrations. 320pp. 5⅜ x 8½.
20610-6

FAIRY AND FOLK TALES OF THE IRISH PEASANTRY, William Butler Yeats (ed.). Treasury of 64 tales from the twilight world of Celtic myth and legend: "The Soul Cages," "The Kildare Pooka," "King O'Toole and his Goose," many more. Introduction and Notes by W. B. Yeats. 352pp. 5⅜ x 8½.
26941-8

BUDDHIST MAHAYANA TEXTS, E. B. Cowell and others (eds.). Superb, accurate translations of basic documents in Mahayana Buddhism, highly important in history of religions. The Buddha-karita of Asvaghosha, Larger Sukhavativyuha, more. 448pp. 5⅜ x 8½.
25552-2

ONE TWO THREE . . . INFINITY: Facts and Speculations of Science, George Gamow. Great physicist's fascinating, readable overview of contemporary science: number theory, relativity, fourth dimension, entropy, genes, atomic structure, much more. 128 illustrations. Index. 352pp. 5⅜ x 8½.
25664-2

EXPERIMENTATION AND MEASUREMENT, W. J. Youden. Introductory manual explains laws of measurement in simple terms and offers tips for achieving accuracy and minimizing errors. Mathematics of measurement, use of instruments, experimenting with machines. 1994 edition. Foreword. Preface. Introduction. Epilogue. Selected Readings. Glossary. Index. Tables and figures. 128pp. 5⅜ x 8½.
40451-X

DALÍ ON MODERN ART: The Cuckolds of Antiquated Modern Art, Salvador Dalí. Influential painter skewers modern art and its practitioners. Outrageous evaluations of Picasso, Cézanne, Turner, more. 15 renderings of paintings discussed. 44 calligraphic decorations by Dalí. 96pp. 5⅜ x 8½. (Available in U.S. only.)
29220-7

ANTIQUE PLAYING CARDS: A Pictorial History, Henry René D'Allemagne. Over 900 elaborate, decorative images from rare playing cards (14th–20th centuries): Bacchus, death, dancing dogs, hunting scenes, royal coats of arms, players cheating, much more. 96pp. 9¼ x 12¼.
29265-7

MAKING FURNITURE MASTERPIECES: 30 Projects with Measured Drawings, Franklin H. Gottshall. Step-by-step instructions, illustrations for constructing hand-some, useful pieces, among them a Sheraton desk, Chippendale chair, Spanish desk, Queen Anne table and a William and Mary dressing mirror. 224pp. 8⅛ x 11¼.
29338-6

THE FOSSIL BOOK: A Record of Prehistoric Life, Patricia V. Rich et al. Profusely illustrated definitive guide covers everything from single-celled organisms and dinosaurs to birds and mammals and the interplay between climate and man. Over 1,500 illustrations. 760pp. 7½ x 10⅛.
29371-8

Paperbound unless otherwise indicated. Available at your book dealer, online at **www.dover publications.com**, or by writing to Dept. GI, Dover Publications, Inc., 31 East 2nd Street, Mineola, NY 11501. For current price information or for free catalogues (please indicate field of interest), write to Dover Publications or log on to **www.doverpublications.com** and see every Dover book in print. Dover publishes more than 500 books each year on science, elementary and advanced mathematics, biology, music, art, literary history, social sciences, and other areas.

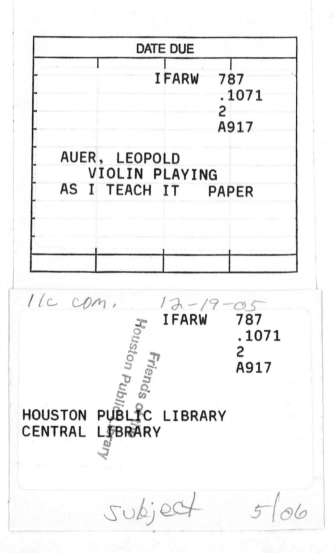